ORIGIN

OF THE

CRITICAL TEXT

A Synopsis of Significant Factors

H. D. Williams, M.D., Ph. D.

THE OLD PATHS PUBLICATIONS, INC.
GOLD FLUME WAY
CLEVELAND, GEORGIA 30528

BIBLE FOR TODAY #3386

Disclaimer

The author of this work has quoted the writers of many articles and books. This does not mean that the author endorses or recommends the works of others. If the author quotes someone, it does not mean that he agrees with all of the author's tenets, statements, concepts, or words, whether in the work quoted or any other work of the author. There has been no attempt to alter the meaning of the quotes; and therefore, some of the quotes are long in order to give the entire sense of the passage.

Library of Congress Control Number: 2008941462
REL006100: Religion: Biblical Criticism & Interpretation

ISBN 978-0-9820608-4-1

All Scripture quotes are from the King James Bible except those verses compared and then the source is identified.

Address All Inquiries To:
THE OLD PATHS PUBLICATIONS, Inc.
142 Gold Flume Way
Cleveland, Georgia, U.S.A.

Web: www.theoldpathspublications.com
E-mail: TOP@theoldpathspublications.com

BIBLE FOR TODAY #3386
Web: www.biblefortoday.org
E-mail: bft@biblefortoday.org

DEDICATION

This year, 2008, my wife and I were blessed with two great grandchildren, Owen Keith and Matthew Scott Williams. We have a prayer for these two precious new souls. When they are old enough to understand, may they be found faithful to the Preserved Words of our Great God and Saviour:

> *Moreover it is required in stewards, that a man be found faithful. 1 Corinthians 4:2*

And so, this work is dedicated to them in anticipation of fulfillment of our prayer.

TABLE OF CONTENTS

CONTENTS	PAGE

ABBREVIATIONS & DEFINITIONS

ABS: American Bible society

Aleph: Sinaiticus MS

B: Vaticanus MS.

Broad Church: a loose alliance of scholars and Anglican priests in England during the 1800s who believed many heretical teachings.

Codices (codex): were writing materials, such as animal hide, bound together at the edge like a book.

Conjectural emendation: one of the tenets of Westcott and Hort for evaluating the MSS of the Bible. It is applying subjectivism to MSS in order to try and determine the Words of God—a foolish and foolhardy approach.

CT: Critical Text or Critical Texts.

DE: dynamic equivalency or dynamic equivalent translating.

DNA: the genetic material, deoxyribonucleic acid that determines the genetic makeup of an individual.

DOTC: the disease of textual criticism, which once exposed to and infected, is most likely not curable.

FunE: functional equivalent translating; it is another name for DE.

Gnostic: someone who believes knowledge leads to salvation and good works. There are many classes of Gnostics such as the **Docetics**, who believed Christ only *seemed* to have 'flesh' because they believed material substance was evil.

Judaizers: the Jews or those sympathetic to Judaism who require believers in Christ to combine the law (works) with grace in order to be saved. They are 'legalists' who require such acts as circumcision, observance of Jewish ordinances, obedience to the Mishna or oral law with all its restrictions.

KJB: King James Bible

Lectionary (lectionaries): codices, organized for Scripture reading in churches on particular days.

Logos: is a word corrupted by Greek philosophers to refer to a *created* being who created the universe. The true Logos is the Lord Jesus Christ who is God and an eternal being.

Majuscules: uncials.

metaphor: "implicit comparison that is used to describe somebody or something by a word or phrase that is not meant literally but by means of a vivid comparison expresses something about him, her, or it, e.g. saying that somebody is a snake; or figurative language that involves figures of speech or symbolism and does not literally represent real things." (e.g. the Lion of Judah, the Lamb of God) (Encarta).

Minuscules: handwritten manuscripts in a cursive-type script (i.e. longhand).

MS: handwritten manuscript.

MSS: (pl.) handwritten manuscripts.

NA: Nestle Aland (NT Greek Text).

NIV: New International Version.

NT: New Testament.

OT: Old Testament.

Papyrus: a paper-like material made from reeds usually found along a river bank such as the Nile and beat into a pulp-like material, dried, and used for paper. It was very perishable except in dry, arid countries such as Egypt where many cults existed. Sometimes, animals hides were used as writing material, but it was very expensive. The manuscript Vaticanus (B) produced from animal hide is a codex presently located in the Vatican library.

Preserved: with a capital "P" refers to the preservation of the original Words of God in Hebrew, Aramaic, and Greek. With a small "p", it refers to the Words of God accurately and faithfully translated into the languages of the world such as found in the KJB (English), RVG (Spanish), and a few others.

Pseudo-epigraphal: MSS (either letters or books) written under a false name.

RT/TT: stands for the Received Texts/Traditional Texts. In this work it will generally stand for the OT and NT manuscripts, occasionally only the Greek 'received' texts. The Masoretic Hebrew texts were received and preserved from and by the nation Israel; Greek texts were received and preserved by the sanctified churches.

RVG: Reina Valera Gomez Spanish Bible

TC: textual criticism.

UBS: United Bible Society (with a superscript it refers to a specific NT Greek Text).

Uncials (or majuscules): are manuscripts written in something like capital letters and the word comes from the Latin, uncia, meaning 'a twelfth part.' Classical books were generally written in this fashion until about the sixth century. Overlapping this time period were the manuscripts written in minuscules (or cursives), which was a script of smaller letters in a running hand. Minuscule comes from the Latin, minusculus, meaning 'rather small.' Otherwise, manuscripts were written in cursive or 'running' hand and were used for rapid writing and non-literary documents (Bruce Metzger, *The Text of the New Testament;* p. 9).

W/H: Westcott and Hort (or Westcoot & Hoot, purposefully misspelled).

PREFACE

Higher and Lower Criticism

The theories of textual criticism (TC) are undermining (1) faith in the preserved WORDS of the Bible and therefore, (2) confidence in a Holy God who honors His promises. He has never failed, but the discipline of TC creates an atmosphere of doubt about an Omniscient, Omnipotent, Omnipresent God. Criticism of the Bible is generally divided into higher and lower criticism. Both disciplines are from the well of unbelief. They are false, subjective, theory-based disciplines. **Higher criticism** questions the authenticity of the historicity of the Biblical text. For example in higher criticism, the Pentateuch, called the "Documentary Hypothesis," is often presented as a late compilation of several authors instead of being recognized as recorded by Moses and affirmed by the Lord Jesus Christ in the NT. **Lower criticism** evaluates the differences between words in manuscripts and attempts to arrive at the correct ones. The problem with each discipline is the subjectivism in their 'constructed' **tenets** and in the **texts** that result from their approach. Objectivism is discarded in favor of 'scholarly interpretation.' Each discipline influences the other to enter into deeper and deeper apostasy and heresy. Higher criticism's origins occurred early in the post-Apostolic era. The heretic Origen from Alexandria, Egypt was a significant theorizer and higher and lower critic of the Scripture (q.v.).

The disciplines exploded in the Reformation, which began the spiral into events and circumstances that led to the construction of the modern Critical Texts. The significant factors contributing to the development of these false texts from these two unprofitable disciplines are: 1. Doubt in God and His inspired, infallible, inerrant, preserved, pure, perfect Words, 2. Belief in a preserved "message" from God instead of reliance upon Words preserved to the *"jot and tittle,"* 3. The resurgence of mysticism associated with New Ageism, Occultism, and Spiritism as a result of false freedom from absolute objective truth, and 4. The renewed interest in humanism (see the Humanist manifesto), atheism, evolution, and the disciplines of science as the answers to man's questions.

God Is Able

Since the beginning of creation of the universe for an inhabitable earth, God has warned that attempts would be made to subvert His intentions and plans for His Words (q.v.). However, the creation with all its complexities (e.g. see DNA, atomic structure, particle and quantum physics, and astrophysics, etc), the literal fulfillment of prophecies in the Bible, the thousands of virtually identical MSS, and the evidence of God's personal involvement in the lives of individuals confirms the truth of precise, preserved, perfect, pure Words being preserved; not just the message, idea, thought, or concept. Our God is the eternally pure, precise, true, just, all-knowing, powerful, present being! He is able!

The theories claiming preservation of the message and not the Words to the very letter and syllable allows man to subjectively change the Words of God, which He intended to be equivalent to a Contract. The words of a legal contract cannot be changed without the permission of both parties. In His Contact, God relates that He will never change the Words (Psa. 12:6-7, 119:89, Mat. 4:4, 24:35, 1 Pe. 1:23-25, etc.). He said:

"Heaven and earth shall pass away, but my words shall not pass away." Matthew 24:35

"For ever, O LORD, thy word is settled in heaven." Psalms 119:89

These verses above are clear. God will make certain that His Words are preserved to *"the jot and tittle"* (Mat. 5:17-18). They will not be *"broken"* (Mat. 5:19, Jn. 10:35).

Damage to the Foundation of the Righteous

Those falling into the trap of TC are on "sinking sand." From the beginning of creation, man has been subtly influenced to accept changes in the Words of God. These changes have reached a crescendo in these last days. They are destroying the foundation of Christian beliefs, and:

> *"If the foundations be destroyed, what can the righteous do?" Psalms 11:3*

It bears repeating that the purpose of the underlying spiritual forces contributing to the undermining of God's Contract is to destroy man's faith in God and His Words. It opens wide the doors to hell.

It is important for believers to understand the origin of textual criticism and the development of modern Critical Texts. Theories have no place for consideration when it comes to something as important as the Words of God and their proper translation.

This book is a compilation of information collected over several years. Much of it can be found in books by this author and others, particularly the books: *The Lie That Changed The Modern World* by H. D. Williams, M.D., Ph.D., *Defending the King James Bible* by Pastor D. A. Waite, Th.D., Ph.D, *The King James Bible Defended* by Edward Hills, Th.D., Ph.D., and Dr. Jack A. Moorman's books, *Forever Settled, Early Manuscripts, Church Fathers, and the Authorized Version,* and *8,000 Differences Between the N.T. Greek Words of the KJB and the Modern Versions.* Many other authors have documented important relevant facts in this struggle. Some of their information is included. All of the authors cannot be mentioned. Many materials are available from Bible For Today (BFT) ministries in Collingswood, NJ. BFT is on the web. Examination of many of these materials has affirmed this author's belief that God preserved His Words as He said He would. **So, how can there be several different original language texts all claiming to be the Words of God?**

The conclusion of this author is that God is allowing duped men, who are influenced by enemy spiritual forces, to reconstruct or change His Contract in order to test the faith of believers and to prove their position and practice in the faith.

> *Mercy unto you, and peace, and love, be multiplied. Beloved, when I gave all diligence to write unto you of the common salvation, it was needful for me to write unto you, and exhort you that ye should earnestly contend for the faith which was once delivered unto the saints. For there are certain men crept in unawares, who were before of old ordained to this condemnation, ungodly men, turning the grace of our God into lasciviousness, and denying the only Lord God, and our Lord Jesus Christ. Jude 1:2-4*

But for those who have gone astray:

"Woe unto them! for they have gone in the way of Cain, and ran greedily after the error of Balaam for reward, and perished in the gainsaying of Core." Jude 1:11

They are truly **"clouds without water"** (Jude 1:12). A cloud without water in it would be 'a hypocritical cloud;' and so, those claiming to trust in the God of the Bible and His inspired, preserved Words, yet who desire to reconstruct them or who accept their reconstruction, are *"clouds without water."* May God have mercy on their souls. Jesus' comments concerning hypocrites should frighten them, if they are believers (cf. Pr. 11:9, 19, Mat. 7:5, 15:7-8, 23:13-29).

The way of the men who are *"clouds without water"* may seem logical, but God repeatedly demonstrates in His Words the foolishness of man. Paul records:

"Where is the wise? where is the scribe? where is the disputer of this world? hath not God made foolish the wisdom of this world?" 1 Corinthians 1:20

One night while preparing this document, I woke up thinking about the Disease of Textual Criticism (DOTC). Some of us were exposed to the disease, but we never contracted DOTC. Others were exposed and contracted it. Those who contracted the DOTC may be cleansed, but they are never cured. This is like "leprosy" in the Bible, which is a metaphor or "type" for sin. Scripture talks about "cleansing of leprosy" similar to "cleansing of sin" in those redeemed and reconciled, but we are never cured of sin until glorification. Another parallel is cancer. People who develop cancer have a disease. They are never cured and must always be careful. They must constantly have exams; probably, because of the oncogene (cancer gene) carried by so many.

The following chart demonstrates the three possible classes of disease carriers. One cannot escape being exposed to DOTC in this modern world of the internet and other means of rapid communication.

The Epidemiology of the DOTC

The Disease of Textual Criticism (DOTC)		
Exposed	Exposed	Exposed
Never Contract the Disease (like Dr. D. A. Waite, David Otis Fuller, Edward Hills)	Contract the Disease, cleansed, but not (never) cured. (Like many men who are in a half-way house, one foot in Textual Criticism and the other out)(e.g. Calvin George, Bob Jones University Faculty). Like Typhoid Mary, who did not realize she had the disease, they can spread the disease to those whose immune system is compromised (immature, still on milk).	Contract the Disease (DOTC), expose and infect many others with it, destroying confidence in God and His Words, and die from it. Metzger Ehrman Westcott Hort and all the rest

Our Bible schools must shield innocent students from exposure to the DOTC, therefore protecting them from possible infection.

Careless Handling of the Bible

The preservation of the Words of God versus the denial of their preservation and the belief that only the "message" or "thought" is preserved have created an atmosphere of lackadaisical, whimsical, careless handling of the Bible.

A couple of examples are necessary. An example is the recent announcement by Thomas Nelson Inc. that they will begin issuing its popular New Living Translation of the Bible minus the minor prophets Amos and Nahum. They reasoned:

> "People just weren't reading them, so it was a fairly
> easy business decision....'We're not saying those
> books aren't part of the canon, it's just that if people
> want to read them they'll have to find them
> elsewhere...'[e]ditors also took their red pens to
> Leviticus, nipping and trimming 'the stuff that has
> absolutely no relevance to modern American life,' says
> Bremley." "Leviticus reads better in abridged form.
> There's more storyline." "A committee is also
> researching the possibility of condensing certain
> 'repetitive psalms,' and merging I and II Kings and I
> and II Chronicles."[1]

Furthermore, executive members of the American Bible Society (ABS) announced that they would begin publishing the Koran in order not to offend Muslims and to show compassion for those converted to Islam. This attack on the Canon of Scripture and political correctness reflects not only the weakness of the current discipline of Bibliology among schools and publishers as a result of higher and lower criticism, it demonstrates the disdain for the very Living Words of a Living God.[2] This is very strange for people who claim they believe in the *"word[s] of life"* (Phil. 2:16). Their attempt to please the reader rather than doing all to God's glory will result in catastrophes of Biblical proportions (Rev. 4:11, 5:12-13). The Apostle Paul cautions the church at Philippi to:

> *"Fulfil ye my joy, that ye be likeminded, having the*
> *same love, being of one accord, of one mind. Let*
> *nothing be done through strife or vainglory; but in*

---

[1] Lark News, Volume 1, Issue 9, Tuesday, September 16, 2008.
[2] H. D. Williams, M.D., Ph.D., *The Attack on the Canon of Scripture* (The Old Paths Publications, Cleveland, GA, 2008).

lowliness of mind let each esteem other better than themselves." Philippians 2:2-3

The phrase, *"let nothing be done through strife or vainglory"* points to those who do things such as taking a penknife to the Scriptures for selfish ambition and conceited pride and as menpleasers (cf. Jer. 36:23, Eph. 6:6,). Hopefully, this brief work will set someone on the path of righteousness; that is, to be right with God and please Him by contentedly receiving His Words and by recognizing the 'origin of the Critical Text.'

In Christ,

H. D. Williams, M.D., Ph.D.

CHAPTER 1

INTRODUCTION

The Origin of Criticism of God's Words

The origin of "criticism" of the Words of God began *"in the beginning"* (Gen. 1:1). The word criticism in this work will mean denigration, censure, condemnation, and corruption. The opposite would be to praise the Words of God without reservation; those Words which are 'received' and 'recognized' and 'preserved' both from the Jews and the sanctified churches (Rom. 3:1-2, 1 Tim. 3:15)

Satan Is The Instigator

Criticism of the Words of God can be found in the Garden of Eden and in the beginning of the earthly ministry of the Lord Jesus Christ (Gen. 1:1-3:7, Mat. 3:1-4:11). Satan, the archenemy of God, instigated the corruption of the Words of God. It has continued throughout the ages by his influence. How else could there be such a coordinated attack on this one book, the Bible, which amazingly has withstood the thundering hammers and clanging chisels without a dent? The Bible is Truth. Those who formulate theories and suppositions about the Bible have never demonstrated a shred of proof. As a matter of fact, archaeology and honest research into the history, origin, and transmission of the Bible has established exactly the opposite of many speculations, conjectures, and hypotheses.

The coordinator of the attacks on the Bible could be no less a person than Satan, *"the angel of light."* The Devil is the father of lies and deceit. Satan understood that if he could destroy confidence in the Words of God he could succeed in his plans to usurp God and assume His throne (Isa. 14, Eze. 28). Those who systematically purpose to undermine reliance on the 'received' Words, whether wittingly or unwittingly, are in the clutches of the Devil. Jesus said:

> *"Ye are of your father the devil, and the lusts of your father ye will do. He was a murderer from the beginning, and abode not in **the truth**, because there is no truth in him. When he speaketh a lie, **he speaketh of his own**: for he is a liar, and the father of it." John 8:44 (cf. Jn. 17:17, 8:32)*

Throughout the centuries, he has been the instigator for the neglect of and purposeful changing, adding to, or subtracting from the Words of God. Duped men and women under the influence of adversarial spiritual forces all over this earth are clinging to false theories put forth as facts. A lie or theory repeated often enough becomes truth in the minds of most men (e.g. evolution). Dean John William Burgon said:

> *"But then further, the Scriptures for the very reason because they were known to be **the Word of God became a mark for the shafts of Satan from the beginning.**"*[3] (HDW, my emphasis)

The Apostle Paul mentions the beguiling of man by Satan's "subtilty." Having studied the issues related to the text of Scripture for many years, I know one thing for certain; the enemy is subtle. We fear that many have fallen victim to his wiles. He corrupts the *"simplicity that is in Christ."* Paul said:

---

[3] Dean John William Burgon, *The Causes of Corruption of the Traditional Text of the Holy Gospels, Vol II* (Dean Burgon Society Press, Collingswood, NJ, original 1896 by the Dean's assistant, Edward Miller from the Dean's notes after his death, republished 1998) p. 12.

"But I fear, lest by any means, as the serpent beguiled Eve through his subtilty, so your minds should be corrupted from the simplicity that is in Christ." 2 Corinthians 11:3

In Dr. D. A. Waite's book, *The Superior Foundation of the King James Bible,* he confirms the instigator of the Critical Text. He says:

"Satan is the master of deceitful doubting and he is the author of all this confusion."[4] (HDW, not my emphasis).

After discussing an apparent lie concerning the denial of the evidence for the word, THEOS (meaning God), in 1 Tim. 3:16, David Cloud reports:

When one is searching out issues pertaining to the Bible, he must never lose sight of the FACT that there is a Devil, and that this Devil has been actively resisting the pure Word of God from the beginning. He is the adversary of God and of God's Truth. We do not make these studies in a climate of spiritual neutrality. It was Dr. Devil in the Garden of Eden who first hissed, "Hath God said?" and instructed and encouraged Eve in twisting, adding to, denying, and changing the words of God."[5]

Unless careful, close attention is paid to Truth, the one disguised as the *"angel of light"* will cleverly allow insertion, deletion, or changing of the Words of God (2 Cor. 11:14) to go unnoticed.

---

[4] Pastor D. A. Waite, Th.D, Ph.D., *The Superior Foundation of the King James Bible* (Bible For Today Press, Collingswood, NJ, 2008) p. 26.
[5] David W. Cloud, *Way of Life Encyclopedia of the Bible & Christianity* (Way of Life Literature, Port Huron, MI, 4th Edition, 2002) 63.

Ultimately, the Devil's influence is the true **origin of the modern Critical Text(s) (CT)**.[6] It is the basis of modern Bible translations.

> "The Critical Text is the basis for the majority of modern Bible translations today. It is currently reflected in the Greek New Testaments of the United Bible Societies text and the Nestle-Aland text. These two texts are now identical in regard to their Greek text, but differ in regard to their critical apparatus (the footnotes discussing the different textual variants). Generally, the Critical Text reflects a textual line called *Alexandrian*, a name that is explained later in this chapter."[7]

The Event Strengthening Biblical Attacks

In modern history, there was one single, very significant event that freed unbelievers to launch an ever increasingly loud chorus extolling the Bible as composed of fables and myths. That occasion was the release of Charles Darwin's *Origin of Species* in 1859. Any student of history can detect the influence this book has had on those rewriting the Bible. As we shall see, two of the most important men in the history of the CT, Westcott and Hort, were influenced by Darwin's suppositions.

Proclamations From Scripture

In this work, the evidence of the *origin of purposeful corruption* of the Words of God will be presented; first, using a

---

[6] This author uses modern critical text**s** (pl.) because there are currently many constructed texts such as the Nestle Aland, United Bible Society, and several majority texts in addition to texts that go by the names of individual 'scholars.'

[7] Dr. Thomas Holland, *Crowned With Glory: The Bible from Ancient Text to Authorized Version* (Dr. Thomas Holland, All Rights Reserved, 2000, ISBN: 0-595-14617-1, From SwordSearcher, Version 5.4.1.2, Broken Arrow, OK) Chapter 2.

Scriptural basis. To be enmeshed in Truth is the road that must be taken **to *avoid*** the power of the great deceiver, the Devil, who is the prince of this world, and who influences and corrupts man's imagination, thinking, conscience, and conduct. Being holy, sanctified, or set aside to God after salvation is dependent upon knowledge of His Preserved[8] Words properly, accurately, and faithfully translated into the languages of the world. The second person of the Trinity, the Lord Jesus Christ, implored the Father, the first person in the Trinity, with these words:

> *"Sanctify them through thy truth: thy word is truth."*
> John 17:17

Furthermore, in order to understand the world and the men who inhabit it, we must first turn to Truth. The Scripture says:

> *"I have more understanding than all my teachers: for thy testimonies are my meditation."* Psalms 119:99

The Two Roads

The testimonies of God loudly proclaim the origin of the Words of God, but careful scrutiny of the text also reveals the origin of the Critical Texts and their evolution. That is, there are two texts mentioned in Scripture. God does not emphasize the false text, but it is there in Scripture. For example, Satan said, *"thou shalt not surely die,"* which is

---

[8] The use of Preserved (with a capital) was instituted by Dr. D. A. Waite, Th.D., Ph.D. to indicate the original Preserved Words in Hebrew, Aramaic, and Greek that lie behind the King James Bible (ie. RT/TT). A small "p" indicates the Words of God preserved by the KJB in English (or accurate and faithful translations of the Preserved Words in other languages).

corruption of God's Words (Gen. 3:4). God does not want to draw attention to a false text, but He cites examples to warn believers and to make certain that they know false words or texts exist (Psa 119:104, 128). The "One" route or "way" is the True Text and the other route is a false, subtle, deceitful text. Man chooses which one to follow. Metaphorically, this is like a fork in the road. We can choose which way to go.

The First Road or Route

The first road or route is the Words of God that the Holy Spirit proclaims *"is the way."*

> *"And thine ears shall hear **a word** behind thee, saying, This is **the way**, walk ye in it, when ye turn to the right hand, and when ye turn to the left." Isaiah 30:21*

The words *"behind thee"* are *"the law"* hidden in your heart that the Holy Spirit uses to instruct a believer:

> *"I delight to do thy will, O my God: yea, thy law is within my heart." Psalms 40:8 Thy word have I hid in mine heart, that I might not sin against thee. Psalms 119:11 Thy testimonies have I taken as an heritage for ever: for they are the rejoicing of my heart. Psalms 119:111*

If our conscience, a part of the soul, is not seared or defiled, the Spirit can use the Words of the "true" route, the law, to influence us to do His will.[9] Recall that on several occasions in Scripture, Jesus used

---

[9] H. D. Williams, M.D., Ph.D., *Hearing the Voice of God* (The Old Paths Publications, Cleveland, GA, 2008). See Chapter 3, The Conscience.

the word, *"law,"* to refer to the entire Old Testament.[10] God places the knowledge of His *"law"* in our hearts. When Jesus and Paul use the word "law" in some passages, I believe that they are referring to the whole Old Testament with its commandments, precepts, judgments, and so on. In the passage to follow, I believe Paul is referring to the moral 'laws' in the Old Testament (Ex. 20:1ff, in addition to protective precepts, commandments, and similar). Also, recall that **"the Old Testament is the New Testament concealed, and the New Testament is the Old Testament revealed"** in many ways. Paul clearly proclaims:

> *"For when the Gentiles, which have not the law, do by nature the things contained in the law, these, having not the law, are a law unto themselves: Which shew the work of **the law written in their hearts**, their conscience also bearing witness, and their thoughts the mean while accusing or else excusing one another;)" Romans 2:14-15*

Along most roads there are road signs. Should we travel the "road" with road signs that affirm His Truth? The road signs along *"the way"* in the "law" (the whole OT) loudly proclaim: *"this is the way, walk ye in it;" "thy word is truth;" "Blessed is the man that walketh not in the counsel of the ungodly, nor standeth in the way of sinners, nor sitteth in the seat of the scornful. But his delight is in the law of the LORD; and in his law doth he meditate day and night;" "the meek will he guide in judgment: and the meek will he teach his way;" "good and upright is the LORD: therefore will he teach sinners in the way; "commit thy way unto the LORD; trust also in him; and he shall bring it to pass;"* and many many similar things.

---

[10] Waite, op. cit., p. 22 *(The Superior Foundation of the King James Bible).*

"Teach me thy way, O LORD; I will walk in thy truth: unite my heart to fear thy name." Psalms 86:11

The Second Road or Route

The second "road" has deceitful signs that loudly proclaim:

1. "conjectural emendation;"

2. "the oldest is the best;"

3. "the shorter reading is correct;"

4. "the longer reading is corrupt;"

5. "there is no intentional corruption in this route;"

6. "the best manuscripts are from Alexandria;"

7. "this is the scholarly way;"

There are many other 'road signs' along this road that rob you of the Truth (q.v.). But the Lord warns: *"For the LORD knoweth the way of the righteous: but **the way of the ungodly shall perish"** (Psalms 1:6). Which road are you on? The way of the righteous or the way of the ungodly?

If you do not accept the fraudulent way of subjectivism, which is what "conjectural emendation" is, the 'scholars,' 'administrators,' or 'princes' along the way of the deceptive road will persecute you.[11]

"Princes have persecuted me without a cause: but my heart standeth in awe of thy word. Psalms 119:161

---

[11] Compare the subjectivism of W/H tenets with Dean Burgon's approach found in *The Traditional Text of the Holy Gospels,* Chapter III, beginning on p. 40 (Dean Burgon Society Press, Collingswood, NJ, originally published, 1896 by Edward Miller, who was Dean Burgon's assistant and he compiled the book, published 1998 by the DBS.

Modern-Day Judaizers

During the days of Paul, the Judaizers were attempting to undermine Paul's teachings and to bring believers under their control. The hoped for result would be bondage to them and to the Law. The modern textual critics are modern-day Judaizers. That is, they are trying to bring the masses under their authority and control by constructing *intellectual conjectural* tenets. According to them, their claims are equivalent to 'law,' which must be obeyed in order to properly approach the manuscript (MS) evidence and arrive at the correct wording of the Scripture. If you do not follow their recommendations and proclamations (their law), you are excluded from their 'sect,' scholarly club, ivory tower, school, university, and favor. Personally, I would rather "seek His face" or His favor (Psa. 105:4)

In effect, the scholars by default become the de facto *"schoolmaster,"* but they do not lead you to the true "law," which is for the purpose *"to bring us to Christ"* (Gal. 3:24). Rather, they lead you to their false laws, which bring you **to them.** The tenets of modern textual criticism, which keep us from *"the faith"* that leads us to the Lord Jesus Christ and His Words (Gal. 3:23-24), are self-serving.

One of the most intriguing accounts in the Scripture is the passage where Paul discusses the typology of Sarah (the "freewoman") and Hagar as it relates to bondage to the law (Gal. 4:21-31). The underlying themes in the passage and its context are (1) the concepts of maturity in Christ and (2) freedom in Christ from bondage to the law.

The "bondmaids" of today are the textual critics who perpetrate bondage to their false beliefs and tenets based on man's philosophy and subjectivism. The children of the modern bondmaid

(Hagar) are those who have rejected *"the faith"* with its clear statements and promises in favor of false texts and their modern translations (e.g. USB/NA Greek texts, NIV, NLB, NASB modern versions). They are duped. They have followed after the modern *"bondmaid"* of textual criticism. They are the modern legalist or Judaizer who adds, subtracts, or changes something in *"the faith."* Changing anything in *"the faith which was once delivered unto the saints"* (Jude 1:3), is the old trick of the serpent to bring someone into bondage to him as opposed to the freedom available in the Creator of all, the Lord Jesus Christ.

The children of the *"freewoman"* (Sarah) are those who live *"by faith"* and believe and trust in Preservation of the Words of God *"according to the scriptures"* and their accurate and faithful preservation in translations such as the KJB and the RVG by superior men of faith, of knowledge, and of wisdom. They do not subscribe to the wisdom of this world (1 Cor. 1:17-31). This is an absolute necessity for true freedom in Christ. As the Scripture says:

> *"Behold, his soul which is lifted up is not upright in him. but the just shall live by his faith." Habakkuk 2:4*

> *"So then faith cometh by hearing, and hearing by the word of God." Romans 10:17*

> *"But without faith it is impossible to please him: for he that cometh to God must believe that he is, and that he is a rewarder of them that diligently seek him." Hebrews 11:6*

> *"Now the just shall live by faith: but if any man draw back, my soul shall have no pleasure in him." Hebrews 10:38*

"But that no man is justified by the law in the sight of God, it is evident: for, The just shall live by faith." Galatians 3:11

"Verily I say unto you, Whosoever shall not receive the kingdom of God as a little child shall in no wise enter therein." Luke 18:17

Certainly, no CT man is justified by his 'law,' no matter how loud or confident he is in his position. His position is flat wrong *"according to the scriptures."*

Questions We Must Ask Ourselves

The questions that all of us must ask of ourselves are these: Are you mature in Christ or are you *"under sin"* and, perhaps unwittingly, under a false *"schoolmaster"?* Are you a child of the bondmaid or of the freewoman? I would like to extend the metaphor used by the Apostle Paul to the current situation concerning the two routes. Typologically, route one is receiving by faith the Words of God that came to us through the churches and the nation Israel (Jn. 17:8, Rom. 3:1-2, 1 Tim. 3:15). A person holding to this route is a child of the "free" route.

Typologically, route two is **not** believing the "promises" of God and therefore coming into bondage under the 'scholars' and their laws or tenets of modern textual criticism. It is a very costly road to follow. The tenets, as we shall see, are from apostate and heretical professors, teachers, and 'scholars.' Their desire is to keep you in their grasps and under their control (q.v.). The reason for their **desire** is similar to the alcoholic or drunk who wants you to drink their poison (alcohol) with them and to remain *"in the flesh."* Paul accused the Judaizers of similar **desires.** In the following verse, one way to understand and apply Paul's accusation to the modern textual situation is to substitute 'textual critics' for "they;" 'in bondage' for "circumcised;" and for "law" identify it with their subjective tenets of textual criticism:

> For neither _they_ themselves who are _circumcised_ keep the _law;_ but **desire** to have you _circumcised,_ that they may glory in your flesh. Galatians 6:13

More questions that every person must ask himself in these last days are: 1. Are you born of the flesh or are you born again after the Spirit (Gal. 4:29)? 2. By faith, are you mature, free and alive under the Words of Christ and His promises?

Surely, you must see that many are in bondage to the 'scholars.' This is dependency on a person other than the Lord Jesus Christ. In these last days, it is a significant character defect. Just look at the celebration by the world of the recent election of Barack Obama to the presidency of the US. He is hailed as a "messiah." Typologically, those dependent on the scholars (and politicians and the world) and their ways are of Mount Sinai and in bondage to scholarly pontifications and legalism and not free through the Words of God. They are **not** part of the _"Jerusalem which is above [that] is free, which is the mother of us all"_ (Gal. 4:26), but rather they are of the earthly _"Jerusalem which now is, and is in bondage with her children."_ (Gal. 4:25). Praise God that we have men who have their part of the 'new' Jerusalem _"without wavering,"_ which one day soon will come down out of heaven (Heb. 10:23, Rev. 2:12).

Hopefully, more and more believers will be renewed and strengthened by the Lord as they live by faith in Him and His Words, just as He empowered Paul and the disciples (2 Cor. 4:7-18). If you are _"born again,"_ you are no longer under a schoolmaster or in bondage to the brokers of false Hebrew and Greek texts. Rather, you are free in Christ and under His Preserved Words.

Scripture Cannot Be Broken

For those of us who *"tremble at his word,"* it is almost an oxymoron to examine the "corrupted Words of God" because God's voice loudly and clearly declares that His Words cannot be corrupted, destroyed, or *"broken"*[12] (e.g. Psa. 12:6-7, Mat. 5:17-19, Jn. 10:35, see the footnote). But some of us who love the Lord Jesus Christ and His (1) precise, (2) preserved, (3) perfect, (4) pure, (5) infallible, (6) indestructible, (7) inerrant, (8) inspired Words, must examine these destructive words to warn our brothers and sisters of the **understated** changes orchestrated through the influence of our subtle enemy. Why do we report these changes as "understated"? Because most modern textual critics proclaim that the subtle changes, in (1) the modern Critical Text of the UBS/NA and (2) the new versions versus (1) the RT/TT and (2) the accurate and faithful translation such as the KJB and RVG, are not important. Do not be fooled. Dr. D. A. Waite and Dr. Jack Moorman have diligently proclaimed and shown that the changes in the modern Critical Text and their translation into the modern quote/unquote "bibles" are **significant.** Dr. Waite points out 156 doctrinal changes in his book, *Defending the King James Bible,* and Dr. Moorman points out 356 in his book, *Early Manuscripts, Church*

---

12 פרר parar a primitive root; to break up (usually figuratively, i.e. to violate, frustrate:--X any ways, break (asunder), cast off, cause to cease, X clean, defeat, disannul, disappoint, dissolve, divide, make of none effect, fail, frustrate, bring (come) to nought, X utterly, make void. λυω luo a primary verb; to "loosen" (literally or figuratively):--break (up), destroy, dissolve, (un) loose, melt, put off.

Fathers, and the Authorized Version, with Manuscript Digests and Summaries.[13]

As we shall see, believers simply need to *recognize* the Words of God. We, as believers, must merely identify the *"good" "way"* (Psa. 25:8, 1 Sam. 12:22-24, 1 Kg. 8:23; only the Lord is good, only His way is good, Mat. 19:17).

But, not only do we have historical (or secular) evidence of men 'breaking' His Words by changing the Words, by adding to them, or by subtracting from them (q.v.), thus disobeying God's commands to "keep" His Words; we have Scriptural evidence also (Nu. 15:31, Isa. 24:5, Jer. 11:10, Eze. 17:19, 44:7, Zec. 11:9-11, and many places). Thankfully, the "broken" Words shall not prevail, but the Words that He preserved shall prevail! As we shall see, they are EASILY recognized. The preserved Words are the starting point to determine by whom and in which locality the corruption began.

Three Important Prerequisites

There are three prerequisites that any reader of this work must accept to fully appreciate what is to follow. **First**, if someone does not accept the inspired, pure, Preserved, inerrant, infallible Received Texts/Traditional Texts Words that lie behind the accurate and faithful translation of them found in the KJB by the spiritual and intellectual translators of 1604-1611, then this work will not be beneficial. **Second**, if someone is to understand the origin of the corrupted modern Critical Text (CT) that is represented by the UBS4 (United Bible Society Text)

---

[13] Pastor D. A. Waite, *Defending the King James Bible* (Bible For Today Press, Collingswood, NJ, 8th printing, 2002) pp. 158-185. J. A. Moorman, *Early Manuscripts, Church Fathers, and the Authorized Version, with Manuscript Digests and Summaries* (Bible For Today Press, Collingswood, NJ, 2005) pp. 119-312.

and the Nestle/Aland[27] (NA) texts, then the progenitor of those texts must be recognized. It is Satan. The CT texts have caused confusion to the point of despair; God is not the author of confusion (1 Cor. 14:33). **Third**, the motives and desires of the men involved in the *"construction"* of these texts is uncovered in the Scripture. Rebellion is the major underlying characteristic of men who *reject* or who fail to *recognize* Preserved Truth found in the majority of MSS. Rebellion is as *"the sin of witchcraft."* It is the rejection of the authority of our God and His Words (Pro. 29:2, Mat. 7:29, 21:27, Jn. 5:27). The Scripture says:

> *"And the LORD said unto Samuel, Hearken unto the voice of the people in all that they say unto thee: for they have not rejected thee, but they have rejected me, that I should not reign over them." 1 Samuel 8:7 "For **rebellion** is as the sin of witchcraft, and stubbornness is as iniquity and idolatry. Because thou hast **rejected the word of the LORD**, he hath also rejected thee from being king." 1 Samuel 15:23 (cf. 2 Kg. 17:15, Psa. 119:36, Jer. 6:13, 8:9, Hos. 4:6, 2 Tim 3:1-7, etc.). (HDW, my emphasis).*

In this work, following the appraisal of Scripture as it pertains to criticism of the Words of God, a review of the origin of the manuscripts (MSS) of the CT and the men involved in constructing the CT will be presented. It will include the significant men, important manuscripts, and the places of origin of the corrupted CT.

Definition of Critical and Non-Critical Texts

A *corrupted* text of Scripture, which is **not** necessarily a *Critical Text*, may arise from *intentional* or *unintentional* changes in Scripture (q.v.). The modern Critical Text is a product of apostate and heretical men who used subjectivism in their approach to evaluation of the MSS of Scripture, particularly the NT, which were originally corrupted by the members of Gnostic cults in the first one to two hundred post-apostolic years. Both Dean John William Burgon and F. H. A. Scrivener believed this was the most damaging period of time for corruption of the NT text.[14]

The Words of God found in the Received Texts (RT or TR) or Traditional Texts (TT), which are noncritical-type MSS, may be *unintentionally* corrupted, but are easily *recognized* by examination and collation of MSS. The *unintentional* scribal errors are easily corrected. Some of the unintentional errors include:

1. "**Haplography**—writing once what should have been written twice.

2. **Dittography**—writing twice what should have been written once.

3. **Metathesis**—an inadvertent exchange in the proper order of letters or words.

4. **Fusion**—the combining of the last letter of the first words with the first letter of the following word, or else of combining two separate words into a single compound word.

5. **Fission**—refers to the improper separation of one word into two.

6. **Homophony**—words of entirely different meaning may sound alike and substituted.

7. **Misreading similar-appearing letters**—dated in history because at various stages of the alphabet development some letters, which later were written quite differently, resembled one another in shape.

8. **Homoeoteleuton**—a Greek term meaning, "having a same ending," and identifies the loss of text that can result when the eye

---

[14] Pastor D. A. Waite, *The Superior Foundation of the King James Bible* (Bible For Today Press, Collingswood, NJ, 2008) p. 42.

of the copyist inadvertently passes over all the words preceding a final phrase that is identical with that which closes the sentence immediately preceding, or immediately following.

9. **Homoeoarkton**—means, "that which has a similar beginning" and involves a similar loss of intervening words, as the eye of the scribe jumps from one beginning to another.

10. **Variants**—based on vowel points only."[15]

There are far more 'received-type' MSS, and the original language MSS in Hebrew, Aramaic, and Greek are **virtually identical**. Most differences are simply spelling errors. They can easily be collated and they are the basis of the RT/TT. The Greek MSS behind the TR/TT amount to ninety-nine percent (99%) of the available MSS. The MSS behind the RT/TT are from many areas of the 'earth' and from many nations with many different languages. The Greek MSS are represented by papyrus, uncials, minuscules (cursives), and lectionaries, which are supported by a variety of MSS in other languages, versions in other languages, and church elder writings. The varieties of evidence for the RT/TT are overwhelming. The men who support or are involved in constructing the CT are either denying, lying, or being duped about the evidence. Dean Burgon said:

> "Variety distinguishing witness massed together must needs constitute a most powerful

---

[15] H. D. Williams, M.D., Ph.D., *The Lie That Changed The Modern World* (The Old Paths Publications or Bible For Today, Cleveland, GA and Collingswood, NJ, respectively, 2004) 182-183. This book is available on Amazon by typing in the name of the book or from www.biblefortoday.org. This author believes that vowel points had to be in the original Hebrew text. See the reports by Dr. Thomas Strouse, Dean of Emmanuel Baptist Theological Seminary, works by the expositor John Gill, and others.

argument for believing such Evidence to be true. **Witnesses of different kinds; from different countries; speaking different tongues:--witnesses who can never have met, and between whom it is incredible that there should exist collusion of any kind:--such witnesses deserve to be listened to most respectfully.** Indeed, when witnesses of so varied a sort agree in large numbers, they must needs be accounted worthy of even implicit confidence... Variety it is which imparts virtue to mere Number, prevents the witness-box from being filled with packed deponents, ensures genuine testimony. **False witness is thus detected and condemned, because it agrees not with the rest.** Variety is the consent of independent witnesses,...

It is precisely this consideration which constrains us to pay supreme attention to the combined testimony of the Unicials and of the whole body of the Cursive Copies. They are (a) dotted over at least 1000 years: (b) they evidently belong to so many divers countries,--Greece, Constantinople, Asia Minor, Palestine, Syria, Alexandria, and other part of Africa, not to say Sicily, Southern Italy, Gaul, England and Ireland: (c) they exhibit so many strange characteristics and peculiar sympathies: (d) they so clearly represent countless families of MSS., being in no single instance absolutely identical in their text, and certainly not being copies of any other Codex in existence,--that their unanimous decision I hold to be an absolutely irrefragable evidence of the Truth."[16]

Dr. Waite said:

"If you are talking about the Textus Receptus of the New Testament we find those manuscripts **virtually identical** one with the other...a seamless garment. There

---

[16] Dean John William Burgon, *The Traditional Text of the Holy Gospels, Vol 1* (The Dean Burgon Society Press, Collingswood, NJ, 1998) 50-51.

are a few spelling differences but other than that not much else."[17]

Furthermore, the few differences **in the RT/TT** are easily identifiable. Speaking about the RT/TT, Dean Burgon said:

"We are there able to convince ourselves in a moment that the supposed 'various reading' is nothing else but an instance of licentiousness or inattention on the part of a previous scribe or scribes, and we can afford to neglect it accordingly. It follows therefore,--and this is the point to which I desire to bring the reader and to urge upon his consideration,--that the number of 'various readings' in the New Testament properly so called has been greatly exaggerated. **They are, in reality, exceedingly few in number**; ..."[18]

The MSS that are the basis of the CT total one percent (1%) of the available MSS. Critical Texts (CT) are composed of any **_purposeful_ alteration or reconstruction** of the Words of God by haters of God, supporters of cultic Gnostic-like premises (Rom. 1:30), heretics, or duped 'scholars.'

In the following chart, which demonstrates the evidence for support of the RT/TT behind the KJB, W/H stands for the MSS supporting the Westcott and Hort or UBS/NA type-texts that underlie the modern versions.[19]

---

[17] Pastor D. A. Waite, Th.D., Ph.D., *Fuzzy Facts From Fundamentalists on Bible Versions,* (The Bible For Today Press, Collingswood, NJ) p. 65.

[18] Dean John William Burgon, *The Causes of Corruption of the Traditional Text, Vol II* (Dean Burgon Society Press, Collingswood, NJ, originally published in 1896 by Burgon's associate, Edward Miller, by printers George Bell and Sons, London) 16.

[19] Pastor D. A. Waite, *Defending the King James Bible* (Bible For Today Press, Collingswood, NJ, 8th printing, 2002) p. 56. This is the source for this chart.

	TOTALS	# of MSS WH/TR	% of MSS WH/TR
Papyrus Fragments	81(88)	13/75	15%/85%
Uncials	267	9/258	3%/97%
Cursives	2764	23/2741	1%/99%
Lectionaries	2143	0/2143	0%/100%
Totals:	5255	45/5210	1%/99%

The modern Critical Texts represented by UBS/NA texts were assembled by manipulation or reconstruction of the Words of God for ulterior motives (q.v., e.g. Westcott and Hort's desire to replace the "villainous Textus Receptus"[20]). The manuscripts of the RT/TT are not purposefully reconstructed texts as is claimed by the men who support the modern Critical Texts. They make spurious claims of recensions such as Lucian's recension in the late three hundreds AD (4th century) for which there is **NO** evidence. 1. Certainly, a church meeting or conference of church leaders to revise the Words of God would be widely reported in early writings by church elders (fathers); 2. certainly, any text(s) revised and different from those revered by the early churches would be rejected; 3. certainly any text known to be corrupted by one man such as "Lucian" would be rejected and ignored. Westcott and Hort asserted that there was a revision by Lucian. However, there are only two Lucians in early church history who could have been the alleged perpetrators of a revised "Bible." One Lucian was an Arian, the other was a secular writer who wrote parodies about the Bible. Neither one would have been recognized by the early church as

---

[20] Williams, op. cit. p. 58 (*The Lie*)..

having the knowledge or the spiritual light necessary to construct a revision. The Lucian revision is pure bunk (nonsense).

The Age of Westcott and Hort Is Over

As we shall see, Westcott and Hort were the main instigators of the fallacious principles of modern textual criticism. Westcott, Hort and others make their claims in order to put forth the "oldest" corrupted MSS as the "best." On the surface, their claims may seem to be logical and correct. However, the theories have been debunked. Even Kurt Aland, one of the famous modern CT men, admits the theories put forth by Westcott and Hort, which are a culmination of the previous textual critic's tenets preceding them, are allegedly no longer given any credence (q.v.). Aland said:

"The age of Westcott and Hort...is definitely over!"[21]

Another CT man, K. W. Clark said:

"The textual history that the Westcott-Hort text represents is no longer tenable in the light of newer discoveries and fuller textual analysis. In the effort to construct a congruent history, our failure suggests that we have lost the way, that we have reached a dead end, and that only a new and different insight will enable us to break through."[22]

The differences between the various 'few' MSS of the CT, representing only 1% of all MSS evidence, are vast (e.g. comparing one with another). The differences between the RT/TT and the CT MSS are

---

[21] Williams, op. cit., 215 (The Lie).

[22] Wilbur Pickering, Th.D., *The Identity of the New Testament Text* (Thomas Nelson Publishers, Nashville, TN, 1980) 97.

enormous (about 8-9%), which is massive when speaking about the Bible. Many 'scholars' try to hide this significant information. Dr. Jack Moorman responded to Dr. Dan Wallace, professor at Dallas Theological Seminary, who tries to lump "all" of the MSS together and who does not point out the differences. Dr. Moorman said the following about Dr. Wallace:

> "Again, Wallace says: "There are over 400,000 textual variants among the N.T. manuscripts. But the differences between the Textus Receptus and the texts based on the best Greek witnesses number about 5000." He should have explained how he arrived at 400,000. Had he gone to the trouble, he would have tacitly revealed a very uncomfortable fact for his position. **A hugely disproportionate amount of the variation is to be found among the relatively few manuscripts supporting the Aleph-B text.** The critical editors, Barbara Aland and Klaus Wachtel admit this:
>
>> "The papyri and majuscules are for the most part individual witnesses: despite sharing general tendencies on the forms of their texts, they differ so widely from one another that it is impossible to establish any direct genealogical ties among them. ("The Greek Minuscule Manuscripts of the N.T.", *The Text of the N.T. in Contemporary Research*, p.46)."[23]

God's Commandment to "Keep" His Words

The alteration of the Words of God cannot and does not come from God nor is it permitted by God. Why? God declares His honor of His Words throughout the Scripture (Deut. 18:19, Psa. 138:2, Isa.

---

[23] Dr. Jack A. Moorman, "A Reply to Dr. Daniel Wallace's 'Why I Do Not Think the King James Bible is the Best Translation Available Today'" (Bible For Today Ministries, Web Article, October, 2005) 5.

59:20-21, Mat. 24:25, etc.); that is, every Word in the Canon of Scripture was God-breathed to the jot, tittle, letter, syllable, word, verse, passage, book, and the whole Bible (2 Tim. 3:15, Mat. 5:17-18, 24:35, Rev. 22:18-19, etc.). However, God expects man to be responsible for their preservation. It would be nothing for God to speak into existence a perfect copy of His Words, but as with all things pertaining to man, He expects man to be accountable.

The nation Israel and the churches of the living God are responsible for "keeping" His Words (1 Tim. 3:15). The Holy Spirit has guided the people of God, who are the priesthood of believers, to recognize and "keep" the Canon of Scripture (Jn 16:13, Jn. 14:15, 21, 1 Pe. 2:9, and many other places). Investigation of the word "keep" in the Old Testament and New Testament quickly reveals the true meaning of statements such as:

"If ye love me, keep my commandments." John 14:15

Why is this repeated so many times in the Bible? Because the Words proclaim the message of God, which is *"the faith"* by which man believes and is sanctified (Jn. 17:19, Rom. 10:17, Jude 1:3). He gave them *"ONCE"* through His prophets and apostles to be recorded for ever (eternally). They are recorded in heaven and on earth (Jude 1:3, Psa. 119:89, Ex. 24:37[24]). Believers are commanded to "keep" them; that is, guard, protect, preserve, watch over, and obey them.[25] Any

---

[24] The word, "write," occurs 92 times, "written," occurs 291 times, "record," and its cognates occurs 43 times. Most of them have to do with the Words of God. This does not include other significant words such as "settled," "remembrance," word(s)," etc.

[25] Kent Brandenburg, Editor, *Thou Shalt Keep Them, A Biblical Theology of the Perfect Preservation of Scripture* (Pillar & Ground Publishing, El Sorbante, CA, 2003) This is an excellent scholarly book discussing the commandment by the Lord to preserve, guard, protect, watch over His Words.

change in the Words will change the message that is the foundation upon which believers depend. The Words will be 'broken' (Mat. 5:19). Leland Ryken said:

> "There is no meaning without words, if we change the words, we change the meaning."[26]

This is why men belonging to the priesthood of believers like Dr. Humberto Gomez and his associates diligently seek to be certain the original Words of God are translated by verbal and formal equivalence. Dr. Gomez understands the Words of God *"are spirit and they are life"* (Jn. 6:63). Martin Luther commented on these concepts when he said the following about John 6:63:

> "Christ did not say of His thoughts, but of **His words**, that they are spirit and life."[27]

Anyone understands the importance of the words in a contract. God's Contract with man (contact = Hebrew bariyth, Strong's 1285; Greek, diatheke, Strong's 1242) is far more important than any contract of man because they are ***"the words of eternal life"*** (Jn 6:68).

This is a VERY simple concept, but it has been twisted by men through the centuries. They reject the concept of precise preserved Words that bring a definite message and claim only the "idea," "thought," "message," or "concept" can be derived from uncertain words. They claim they have to do this because the words of the Bible are **not** "all" certain. They claim the "message" is generated by uncertain words; thus necessitating the search for the "lost" precise words, which, when found, demands reconstruction of the text. By

---

[26] J. I. Packer *et al., Translating Truth, The Case for Essentially Literal Bible Translation* (Crossway Books, Wheaton, IL, 2005) 69.
[27] Ibid. 60 (Translating Truth).

using their method of utilizing "all" the MSS, even the ones shown to be corrupted (the 1% of MSS, q.v.), they must subjectively choose the words and thus the words become *"lying words"* and *"chaff" (Isa. 32:7, Jer. 7:4, 8, 23:28). Intentionally* corrupted MSS incorporated into the alleged Bible, become the thoughts of man (Jn. 17:8). And, their premise of "uncertain" and "lost" words is incompatible with the clear literal statements in Scripture.

Furthermore, those responsible for the CT do not believe in perfect Preservation of the **Words** (note the "s") of God as He promised. Therefore confidence in the doctrine, message, thought, idea, or concept is relative instead of complete or absolute. Their liberty in Christ is abandoned for moral and civil "relativity" and ultimately for bondage to man's words and ways. They throw away the liberty in Christ (Heb. 2:17) which is determined by precise, inspired, preserved commandments. God calls their "Idea," "thoughts," etc. *"lying words"* from *"the wicked"* (Psa. 10:1-7, Jer. 7:8, 29:23, etc.).

The false claim of imperfect preservation of the Words of God allows evil men to justify alteration, interpretation, and translation of Scripture for their own purposes, whatever THEIR purpose might be. Furthermore, even though they espouse "inspiration" of the Words of God, they really mean that only the thought, idea, concept, or message is inspired.

Final Authority

What is the significance of these things? It relates to who or what is the final authority. The authority of Scripture is lost if perfect Preservation and plenary inspiration is denied; thus man's philosophy determines and influences his doctrine. The result is freedom from precise doctrine and commandments because the Words of God are no longer a precise contract determined by precise words. They claim the words are not known with certainty. The Bible clearly says that this is not true (Pro. 22:20-21). This is the reason for so many warnings in Scripture to anyone who would alter them (Deut. 4:2-6, Pro. 30:5-6, Rev. 22:18-19). These are simple concepts that are necessarily denied by evil men with ulterior motives who are influenced by Satan and the fallen angels who serve him (Rev. 12:7-9). All too frequently, many men are entangled in corrupted words whether knowingly or unknowingly.

The Influence On Translating

Furthermore, the neglect of the Scriptural mandates related to preservation and of the simple concepts presented above leads to a permissive attitude among many translators of the Words of God. The lenient, liberal interpretation of the "message" or "thought" or "idea" has led to dynamic equivalent (DE) linguistics and translation methods. It has produced corrupted books called 'bibles.' DE translating is of paramount significance in the march toward ecumenism and the emerging church. This is not just a misunderstanding; it is a travesty of unequaled parallel that has helped lead to abandonment of precise doctrines, commandments, and precepts of God. We are "free" in Christ, but that freedom does not release us from doctrinal fundamentals and Scriptural restrictions (Rom. 6:1, 1 Cor. 7:21-23, Gal. 5:18-21). Unfounded freedom, supposedly based on the principles of Scripture, has led to permissiveness in morals, beliefs, ethics, ideologies, philosophies, and doctrines (e.g. the emerging church and decadent societies). Must we be reminded:

A little leaven leaveneth the whole lump. Galatians 5:9

Subsequently, the neglect of the principles given by the Prince from heaven has led to world-wide greed, fornication, and desire for power. We are beginning to see the world-wide economic results of freedom from Scriptural principles and the destruction of confidence in the Words of God, which is His Contract. The consequence has recently led to a call for one currency for the world.[28] This is rapidly leading to ecumenism in all institutions of man, including the ecumenical emerging church. Obviously, these things will lead to the call for a one-world leader and a one-world religion. Over time, it will end in the catastrophe of Biblical proportions that is so clearly outlined for us in the prophetic books of the Old Testament and the Apocalypse (e.g. Rev. 13; 18).

Improper Translating Also Corrupts

If someone understands the necessity of precise Words from a Holy God's Contract delineating the direction for *"the way of life,"* (Pro. 6:23, 10:7, 15:24, 21:8), how can anyone subscribe to modernistic dynamic equivalent translating and linguistics? DE is only an approximation of the Words of God by interpretation, which can and usually does "miss the mark." Change the words and you change the message. DE is not precise or faithful to the Words of God. A "so-called" 'bible' produced by modernistic DE translating does not retain

---

[28] "Reuters |Sep 17, 2008 BEIJING (Reuters) China paper urges new currency order after "financial tsunami. Threatened by a "financial tsunami," the world must consider building a financial order no longer dependent on the United States, a leading Chinese state newspaper said on Wednesday." Some newscasters have recently reported that France is also calling for a one world currency.

the precision and accuracy of verbal and formal equivalency (FE).[29] It is NOT faithful to the Words of God and cannot be called "the Words of God" in a receptor-language (e.g., the KJB and RVG can be said to be the Words of God in English or Spanish). A DE translated book should not be called a Bible. It **perhaps** could be called "a reference book," which *contains* some of the Words of God.

Men who use DE [or functional equivalent (FunE) translating] claim their primary concern is for the "receptor" of **their** translation. In other words, a translation must be perfectly clear to the reader, even if it means altering the precise Words. Functional equivalent (FE) or verbal, plenary translating is at the opposite pole; its purpose is to glorify God by glorifying His Words through precise accurate and faithful translating of them. If an individual is influenced by a heretical or Gnostic-type cult, whether ancient or modern, he will have no reticence about adding to, subtracting from, or changing the "*jot and tittle*" of God's Words. He has come under the influence of Satan. He exalts and glorifies man and "himself" rather than God and His Words.

Truth Supersedes Emotions and Desire

An individual under the influence of Satan may think that his aim is lofty, important, and ideal, but under the scrutiny of the Scripture, it fails. Any man, and especially any believer, must use the precise Words of the Contract to determine the "righteousness" of his actions. Emotions must not be the leading determinate or guide.

The Apostle Peter encountered the travesty of emotions. He thought his lofty motive and desire to prevent the death of the Lord

---

[29] Rev. Dennis Kwok & Faculty of Far Eastern Bible College, *VPP of the Bible, A Course on the Doctrine of Verbal Plenary Preservation* (The Old Paths Publications, Cleveland, GA, 1008). A good course.

Jesus Christ, who is *"the Word of God,"* on the Cross was right (Mat. 16:21, Jn. 1:1-2, 14). But, the motive was not the will of God and therefore, it was the will of Satan. Humanly speaking, it would seem Peter's motive was admirable. But, the Lord Jesus Christ made it perfectly clear that his motive was influenced by Satan (Mat. 16:21-23).

Complicity With The Perpetrators

A person who intentionally changes or corrupts, who is in complicity with the methods and techniques that result in false original language words, false translating, or false Scripture, is in sin. He has lost the call to *"become as little children"* and to *"humble himself as this little child"* (Mat. 18:3-4). He has lost the trust and belief in, and understanding of, the Words of the Holy One, which clearly caution against such a travesty. This abhorrence of God's call by man is exactly what we see in many passages throughout the Bible and in the recorded secular history of man. First, the evidence in the Bible.

Scriptural Demonstration
Of These Principles

First, let us examine some of these principles in Scripture because believers are "people of the book."

"The Roman emperor Diocletian (AD 245 – 313) decreed in AD 303 that every Bible should be destroyed. He had been told that if he could destroy the Bible he would destroy Christianity because **'Christians are a people of the Book.'** Feeling he had succeeded, Diocletian raised a column with the inscription in Latin saying, ' the name of Christian is extinguished.' In AD 312, (emperor) Constantine succeeded him and replaced all the pagan symbols with the symbol of the cross. This remarkable change took place in less than ten years."[30]

In The Garden

God said:

> *"And the LORD God commanded the man, saying, Of every tree of the garden thou mayest freely eat: But of the tree of the knowledge of good and evil, thou shalt not eat of it: for in the day that thou eatest thereof **thou shalt surely die**."* Genesis 2:16-17 (HDW, my emphasis).

Satan, a created angel, rebelled against God (Eze. 28:15ff, Isa. 14:12ff). He did not humble himself; he was prideful; he said, *"I will"* exalt my throne above the throne of God (Mat. 18:4, Isa. 14:12ff) and he purposed to change the Words of God that emanated from the throne of God (Gen. 3:1ff, Psa. 119:89, Mat. 4:4, Jn. 1:1-2, 6:41). The serpent said to Eve in the Garden:

> **"Yea, hath God said"** *Gen. 3:1* (HDW, my emphasis).

> **Ye shall *not* surely die:"** *Gen. 3:5* (HDW, my emphasis; Satan added "not").

Satan's words directly contradicted the Words of God in these passages in Genesis. The devil used the same method in the wilderness temptation of the Lord Jesus Christ. He did not use word-for-word presentation of Scripture, but corrupted the Words of God in both passages by: 1. using dynamic equivalent (DE) translation and 2. by changing the Words. Satan gave his interpretation by saying:

---

[30] Rev. Dennis Kwok and The Faculty of Far Eastern Bible College, *(VPP of the Bible, A Course on the Doctrine of Verbal Plenary Preservation)* The Old Paths Publications, Cleveland, GA, 2008) 27.

"For God doth know that in the day ye eat thereof, then your eyes shall be opened, and ye shall be as gods, knowing good and evil." Genesis 3:5

The chant of New Agers is *"ye shall be as Gods, knowing good and evil."* Consult any book on the New Age and see if this is not true. DE translators effectually are guilty of the same mantra. They interpret the Words of God, as if *they* were God, and change the precise message by subtracting, adding to, or changing the Words, or the order of the Words. Therefore the emphasis, message, and "signification" or meaning of the Words in a passage is transformed through interpretive translating. DE translations invariably claim greater **"light"** results from their translations because they are easier to understand. The Scripture reports Satan was transformed into an "angel of **light**." His ministers among the men of earth claim that their **"light"** from DE translations will lead to righteousness.

"And no marvel; for Satan himself is transformed into an angel of light. Therefore it is no great thing if his ministers also be transformed as the ministers of righteousness; whose end shall be according to their works." 2 Corinthians 11:14-15

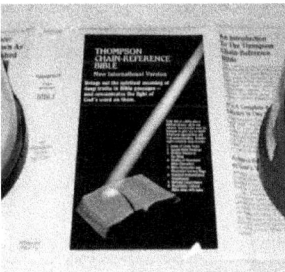

To clearly demonstrate these principles, here is a picture this author took of the cover jacket of an NIV 'bible.' Since you may not be able to read the print, here is what it says:

*"New International Version: Brings out the spiritual meaning of deep truths in Bible passages — and concentrates the **light** of God's word*

on them. Truly this is a Bible ... to give you in-depth
Scriptural appreciation and true understanding." [31]
(HDW, my emphasis).

It is hoped that the vain words of men, who are the children of
disobedience, would be set aside. It is hoped that the true **light** of God,
which only comes from His Preserved Words accurately and faithfully
translated into the languages of the world, would be used. We must
measure all things by the "rule" or Canon or Words of God (1 Cor.
10:13). Paul says:

> *"Let no man deceive you with vain words: for because*
> *of these things cometh the wrath of God upon the*
> *children of disobedience. Be not ye therefore*
> *partakers with them. For ye were sometimes*
> *darkness, but now are ye light in the Lord:* **walk as**
> **children of light***:" Ephesians 5:6-8*

The "**light**" comes only from His Words; light does not
emanate from the lying, vain words of man placed into a text by DE,
nor by removing or changing His Words in order to strengthen false
doctrine and beliefs. It appears that every *"wind of doctrine"* and every
"lust" of the heart that comes along stimulates the craving of men to
translate the Bible to fit their particular desire because of their
"ignorance," "the blindness of their heart," "greediness," and *"lust."*
(Eph. 4:18-19). Greediness refers to "extortion" of men for money
secondary to lust. The word, greediness, is translated from the Greek,
pleonexia, meaning extortion or fraudulency.

The hope of born-again, sanctified men waiting for the return
of our Lord is:

---

[31] *New International Version* (B. B. Kirkbride Bible Co., Inc Indianapolis, IN,
Zondervan Bible Publishers, Grand Rapids, MI, 1983, NIV, 1978) This is a
quotation from the jacket of the book.

"That we henceforth be no more children, tossed to and fro, and carried about with every wind of doctrine, by the sleight of men, and cunning craftiness, whereby they lie in wait to deceive;" Ephesians 4:14

In The Wilderness Temptations

In the wilderness temptations of our Lord, *"the tempter"* or Devil did the same thing that he did in the Garden (Mat. 4:1ff). He either changed the Words or gave an interpretation that suited his purposes. In this passage, the Devil changed the Words by removing some, and therefore, changed their meaning or 'signification' in three passages that allude to the three basic sins: (1). *"lust of the flesh,"* (2) *"lust of the eyes,"* and (3) *"pride of life"* (1 Jn. 2:16). The order we will follow is the order of the temptations in Matthew, which is slightly different. Of course, the underlying determinant of the three basic sins in the book of 1 John is covetousness (Ex. 20:7, Rom. 7:7, 1 Tim. 6:10, 2 Pe. 2:3, 14-15).

Lust of the Flesh

First, the Devil appealed to Jesus' hunger and fatigue after forty days and nights of fasting. Satan appealed to Jesus as a man; exegetically, he was not tempting Jesus as God. This appeal is described by the Apostle John as *"the lust of the flesh"* (1 Jn. 2:16-17). He said to Jesus:

"If thou be the Son of God, command that these stones be made bread." Mat. 4:3

In other words he was saying: 'if thou, **man**, be the Son of God,' make these stones into bread in order to live and not die from hunger. Satan was asking the man, Jesus, to perform a miracle similar to the manna that came down out of heaven from God for the nation Israel during their wilderness experience (Deut. 8:3). Satan forgot that *"he whom God hath sent speaketh the words of God: for God giveth not the Spirit by measure unto him."* (John 3:34).

Obviously, changing the stones to bread was not the will of God. Jesus came to do the will of God (Jn. 5:30). Jesus used Scripture, and He used *"all the words"* recorded in the Old Testament passage, to defeat *"the tempter"* (Ex. 24:4, Deut. 27:3).

> *"But he answered and said, It is written, Man shall not live by bread alone, but by every word that proceedeth out of the mouth of God."* Matthew 4:4 (cf. Deut. 8:3)

The **source** of the manna (food), God, and **the Words of God** are FAR MORE IMPORTANT than bread (food). The *true* bread for man is the Words of God *from Him*, which were *"for ever...settled in heaven"* (Psa. 119:89).

Without a doubt, *"the lust of the flesh"* is a prime reason for men to argue about the Words of God. It is the lust for power and mammon, or greed for money, which can buy 'things' that satisfy the flesh. The proof of this is the number of new English versions of the "bible" available in the market place. Each new version's ad makes the claim to be the best (q.v.); that is, it is the most up-to-date and easiest to understand. For example, the flap covering of *The Everyday Bible, New Century Version,* alleges:

> "Originally, the Bible was written in the languages of common people—so everyone could read and understand. Yet language has changed, and words that were once easily understood often make little sense to us today.

"The Everyday Bible is a new translation that everyone can understand. While it is accurate to the original Hebrew and Greek manuscripts,..."[32]

And on the inside of the version in the Preface, it says:

"The Everyday Bible is an edition of the New Century Version, which is a translation of God's Word from the original Hebrew and Greek languages."[33]

The version never reveals **which** of the several texts claiming to be the "original Hebrew and Greek" words were used. One verse in the *EveryDay Bible* was checked, John 6:47. The correct Greek MSS have:

*Verily, verily, I say unto you, He that believeth **on me** hath everlasting life. John 6:47*

This version, *The Everyday Bible,* has:

"I tell you the truth. He who believes has eternal life."

Believes in what? Has faith in what? Himself? Buddha? Mohammed? (Isa. 53:6, Mat. 7:21-23, Rom. 3:23, 2 Tim. 3:2). Those two words, *"on me,"* (Jn. 6:47), are in the RT/TT, but omitted in the CT.

The 'new' English versions average one being published every six months.[34] This is appalling when so many language-groups or dialects around the world either do not have a translation, do not have enough copies to go around, or do not have a version based upon the Received Texts

---

[32] *The Everyday Bible* (Word Publishing, Dallas, TX, 1988, New Century Version) Flap covering and Preface.

[33] Ibid. (The Everyday Bible).

[34] Ray Van Leeuwen, "We Really Do Need Another Bible Translation" (*Christianity Today*, Oct. 22, 2001).

or Traditional Texts. Why are there so many English versions? Obviously, many persons in English speaking countries have discretionary income that can be spent on the alleged *"newest and best"* version of the Bible. The authors, companies, publishers, and printers of the 'new' versions acquire more "gold" to place in their coffers. This is *"the lust of the flesh."* It is not the will of God (Mat. 28:18-20, Acts 1:8, Rom. 10:13-17).

One reason the verses in Matthew chapter four were given to us by the Holy Spirit was to demonstrate the result of the subtle changing of the words by the Devil. The outcome was that the "signification" or meaning of the words was compromised. Remember, change the Words and you change the message. These types of changes have been the plan of enemy spiritual forces. They have continued. It will go on throughout the days of man's history on this planet. The consequences have been loss of confidence in the Words of God, confusion, and failure of men to follow righteous standards for their protection.

> *"For whatsoever things were written aforetime were* ***written for our learning****, that we through patience and comfort of the scriptures might have hope."* Romans 15:4

This is obviously the reason God is so adamant throughout the Scriptures about 'keeping' and 'preserving' (Greek, *tereo*) His Words. A poor understanding of the Scriptures, secondary to poor exegesis of corrupted Words, is rampant among those who claim to be "Christians," and accordingly, members of the priesthood of believers. If they cannot understand the simple Words in the verses to follow (below), then there is a great problem recognizing *"they* [the Words] *are spirit and they are life."* They are *"the words of eternal life"* (Jn. 6:68).

The reason they do not appropriate or understand the Words may be the same explanation for why "the devils also believe," **but** they are not saved (James 2:19). James 2:20 explains the reason. Devils do not have **faith** (believe and trust). The devils do not have good works or fruit because even though they believe in the existence of God, they do not trust Him. Therefore, they do not have, or do not "do," works that are pleasing to God. That is, they do NOT the will of God, which is the natural outcome of salvation and understanding the inspired Words of God (cf. Eph. 2:8-9, 2 Tim. 3:16-17).

They do not believe in, teach, or support the Preservation of the Words of God to the jot and tittle as described and promised in the Words of God. As a matter of fact, the devils (evil fallen angels or spirits) are behind their corruption, just as their commander, Satan, corrupted God's words in the passages in Genesis chapters 2 and reported in chapter 3 and here in Matthew chapter 4. The commander of devils is a liar (Jn. 8:44).

Neither do many 'scholars' believe in their Preservation to *"the jot and tittle."* For example, Eugene Nida was on the UBS committee, which utilizes the UBS Greek texts (there are now four editions) reconstructed from old corrupted MSS. Nida said:

> "Some phrases in the King James Version are almost impossible to understand correctly **since the Greek text which was available in the seventeenth century was so obviously faulty.**"[35]

The Greek text from the 17th century that Nida references is the RT/TT. It was and is not faulty! It is the preserved Words of God.

Many scholars believe in the Word of God, but not the **Words** of God (note the singular, *word,* versus the plural, *words*). They

---

[35] Eugene A. Nida, *God's Word In Man's Language* (Harper & Row, Publishers, NY, NY, 1952) 72. Eugene Nida was an editor of the United Bible Society's Greek Text along with Bruce Metzger, Matthew Black, Roman Catholic Archbishop Carlo Maria Martini, Allen Wikgren, and Kurt Aland.

proclaim the message, concept, idea, or thought is preserved, but not the Words; that is why they use the singular of word. This cannot be said enough times in order to emphasize their 'uncertainty' about the Preserved Words. This is also the reason that we encounter translations that are man's messages, secondary to DE, which is also called functional equivalent (FunE) translating. DE translators do not believe in jot and tittle Preservation. Therefore, they permit themselves to give their "interpretation" of the "message" and call it a Bible. This is irreverence toward a Holy God and His Holy Words.

Pride of Life

The second temptation that Satan used, in the wilderness experience of Jesus, attempted to appeal to the man Jesus' *"pride of life."* Satan left out God's Words in this temptation. The Devil said:

> *"And saith unto him, If thou be the Son of God, cast thyself down: for it is written, He shall give his angels charge concerning thee: and in their hands they shall bear thee up, lest at any time thou dash thy foot against a stone."* Matthew 4:6

What did he leave out? He left out the following Words: *"in all thy ways,"* **and** added these words *"at any time"* (Psa. 91:11-12).

You may ask why these Words are important. It is because they allude to all the *"ways"* of God, i.e., the will of God. God's ways are: (1) His revealed will (i.e. the God-breathed Words inscripturated, 2 Tim. 3:15-16) and (2) his "secret" will (Deut. 29:29). In other words, there may be a time when God wants the Lord Jesus Christ to "dash" his foot or heel (Gen. 3:15), or to suffer injury, or even death, as on the Cross. When you change the Words of God, you change the message, as in

Matthew 4:6. The "way" or will of God would be subverted to the will of Satan if Jesus had succumbed to the Devil's appeals. (Jn. 1:14, 3:18).

How many 'scholars' can you think of who have not understood that preservation of *"every word that proceedeth out of the mouth of God,"* refers to the revealed will of God? There are many. They have succumbed to the will of Satan. They have been overcome by temptation (Mat. 4:7) (q.v.).

Lust of the Eyes

The third basic sin that the Apostle John designated is *"the lust of the eyes"* (1 Jn. 2:16-17). This is characterized in the book of Matthew in the wilderness temptation of the Lord Jesus Christ by Satan's appeal to the man, Jesus, *"the begotten Son of God,"* to desire all the kingdoms of the world. The Devil *"showed"* Jesus *"the kingdoms of the world and the glory of them"* from an *"exceeding high mountain."* This last appeal by the enemy is the basic appeal to the 'scholars' who desire *"to be as gods"* (Genesis 3:5). They believe, like Satan, that they can exalt THEIR words and *"be as gods"* usurping the authority and position of the Almighty God of Abraham, Isaac, and Jacob. Ultimately, this is a desire for power and a need to be worshipped (Mat. 4:9). Many of us have been exposed to ivory tower 'scholars' or academics who: (1) are proclaiming their words, which have been constructed by textual criticism, as the Words of God, who, by the way, (2) are influencing thousands of students, and who (3) are desirous of being worshipped like Satan. They claim THEIR words are the correct message from God; they completely ignore the numerous places in Scripture that proclaim the Preservation of the Words of God through the institutions, methods, and ways of God (Rom. 3:1-2, 1 Tim. 3:15). Paul clearly warned of this travesty. He said:

> *"That ye be not soon shaken in mind, or be troubled, neither by spirit, nor by word, nor by letter __as from us__, as that the day of Christ is at hand."* 2 Thessalonians 2:2

And in another place, he reported on the corruption of the Words of God. He said:

> *"For we are not as many, __which corrupt the word of God__: but as of sincerity, but as of God, in the sight of God speak we in Christ."* 2 Corinthians 2:17 (HDW, my emphasis)

Notice, Paul said *"MANY"*!

This is the pattern through the ages; MANY individuals altering of the Words of God so that a different message, concept, idea, or thought is presented.

An Example

This calls for a closer examination of the corrupted verse previously presented that was found in the *Everyday Bible*. There are thousands, but one verse should suffice:

> *"Verily, verily, I say unto you, He that believeth on me hath everlasting life."* John 6:47

The New International Version, which also leaves out *"on me,"* has the following words:

> *"I tell you the truth, he who believes has everlasting life."* John 6:47

The evidence supporting the words, *"on me,"* is vast. Dr. Jack Moorman, a manuscript and Biblical text scholar, reports in *Early Manuscripts, Church Fathers, and the Authorized Version, with Manuscript Digests and Summaries*:[36]

AV	NIV
John 6:47	
Verily, verily, I say unto you, He that believeth **on me** hath everlasting life.	I tell you the truth, he who believes has everlasting life
A C-2 D E F G H K M S U V Gamma Delta Lambda Pi Psi Cursives: Majority fam 1, 13 Old Latin: a aur b c d e f ff2 q rl Vulg Syr: peh harc Cop: sa bo pbo Goth Arm-usc Eth Also extant in T Y Omega 047 055 0141 0211 0233	P66 Aleph B C* D L T W Theta pc j ach2 Arm-zoh

Overwhelming Evidence

Without consideration of church elder writings, it is very obvious that MSS evidence alone is overwhelming. Then why did the NIV and other versions leave *"on me"* out? It is related to CT scholars unilaterally claiming: "the oldest is best." According to them, only those few MSS they claim are the best are to be followed [e.g. Vaticanus (B), their favorite, or Sinaiticus (Aleph)]. They selectively disregard any significant information from other well qualified individuals and excellent sources about their "oldest and best" MSS (i.e. that the MSS they use are intentionally corrupted). For instance, it is widely known that church elder (or father) writings contain significant information,

---

[36] J. A. Moorman, *Early Manuscripts, Church Fathers, and the Authorized Version, with Manuscript Digests and Summaries* (Bible For Today Press, Collingswood, NJ, 2005) 210.

quotes, and explanations for changes in the Words of God resulting from cultic and Gnostic activity. Many church elders before 325 AD, such as Irenaeus (c. 120-192) and Tertullian (c. 150-220), wrote against the heresy of cults and Gnostic groups who corrupted the Words of God (2 Cor. 2:17, 2 Thess. 2:2)[37]

Excluded Evidence

Furthermore, the "so-called" late MSS of the RT/TT route are disdained and even not considered by CT scholars. For example, CT authors Drs. Kurt and Barbara Aland in 1981 admitted that

> "attention is now concentrating on the data of patristic citations and of the papyri, but planning and preparations are under way for the addition of new minuscules among the **"constant witnesses"** and a more extensive consideration of the lectionaries, together with **omitting the witness of uncials with a purely Byzantine text.**"[38]

Minuscules and Uncials are defined later in this work. In spite of their declarations, the RT/TT manuscripts **are** "constant witnesses" that are attested by **earlier** MSS than the MSS upon which the CTs are based. Many men, such as Dean Burgon, have pointed out this significant fact, but it has been ignored (q.v.).[39] Furthermore, studies of the critical apparatus of UBS4 and the Nestle/Aland27 texts has demonstrated a selective "omitting" of facts or information in the

---

[37] For example, Irenaeus wrote *"Against Heresies" (Adversus Haereses)* in addition to many other works and Tertullian wrote *"Apologeticus"* among many other writings.

[38] Kurt Aland and Barbara Aland, *The Text of The New Testament, Revised and Enlarged* (William B. Eerdmans Publishing Company, Grand Rapids, MI, 2nd Edition, 1981, English translation, 1989) 36

[39] See Dean Burgon's *Revision Revised* as just one example.

formation of their constructed text. This is similar to selective exclusion of evidence from witnesses in the court room that would change the verdict.

Is there prejudice in the CT route? There is, without a doubt, and there is obvious evidence that can be uncovered in the materials of Kurt and Barbara Aland, Bruce Metzger, Bart Ehrman, F. Clark, and others.

Evidence for Subjectivism

At the 23rd Annual Meeting of the DBS in Ramsey, Minnesota in 2001, Dr. Gary LaMore reported on the apostate Bruce Metzger's comments concerning the UBS Greek texts and decisions related to variants. Metzger said:

> "...a majority of modern textual scholars consider patristic evidence, so long as it stands alone, to count for **almost nothing** in ascertaining the original text...Accordingly, it is only when patristic evidence coincides with the evidence of the Greek manuscripts, or with some unmistakable indication in the early versions, that any stress can be laid upon it. But whenever this is the case, it rises at once into great importance...we have found not reason to abandon the view that, in the nature of the case, it is the Greek manuscripts which provide direct evidence for the text of the New Testament, whereas the versions and if one looks at the footnotes and observes whether readings supported by **Aleph [ℵ] and/or B [Vaticanus]** are preferred or rejected, **to a very large degree they are preferred, not rejected.** In fact, there are few texts on which Aleph and B agree that do not end up to be the preferred reading; and also there are few preferred readings that do not have the

support of either Aleph or B or one of their corrected forms, so to speak."[40]

In other words, if church elder writings are in agreement with the modern CT then they are accepted, but if they do not agree, then they are discounted.

Duped Believers Change the Words of God

The arguments of men supporting CT prerogatives or tenets have led even many alleged "Bible-believing" individuals to proclaim "message preservation" as opposed to Preservation of the Words of God. They proclaim that they are "Bible-believers," who believe in the inspiration of the Words of God, but fail to give deference to the promises found in Scripture that proclaim Preservation as well.

They report belief in the virgin birth, death, resurrection, and ascension of the Lord Jesus Christ based upon the Words in Scripture. Yet, they do not believe in the Preservation of the Words of God as promised in those same Words. The incongruity is inexplicable to many of us. Those who proclaim "message" preservation (i.e., they are opposed to perfect word Preservation) are 'critically' wrong. They are duped. They are being influenced by Satan through a very common technique. It is the practice of appealing to pride through related, but distinct separation of concepts. They are choosing which words to believe and which words to either throw out or twist to fit their beliefs. An example is necessary.

A common characteristic of believers who corrupt the Words of God is their appeal to a singular attribute or character trait of God; that

---

[40] Dr. Gary E. La More, Ph.D., D.D., "UBS[23] Compared With UBS[24]" (Dean Burgon Society Message Book, Collingswood, N.J., 2001) p. 60.

is, they elevate the attribute of love above any other attribute of God. They emphasize the necessity of getting the "message" of God (i.e. the message of love) to the world, which is important, but not if it is not proclaimed through the VERY Words of God. Those very Words of God also declare the judgment of God, which they consistently fail to mention. God's judgment of sin led to the death of His Son on the Cross that He might be the just and justifier (Rom. 3:26). God's judgment of an individual's sin will lead to eternal damnation unless they appropriate God's gospel which demands repentance and belief in His Son's proclamation that eternal life is predicated on *"believeth on me"* (Jn. 6:47). God's love does not allow belief in any other way to God, such as found in Buddhism, New Ageism, or merely the claim that "he is a man of faith" (Jn. 14:6). Faith in what? Many evangelicals have been influenced by corrupted texts to believe that anyone can be saved who "believes." They claim it is NOT necessary to know or believe specifically in the Lord Jesus Christ. Concerning the subject of salvation, Billy Graham said:

> "Those are decisions only the Lord will make…I believe the love of God is absolute. He said he gave his son for the whole world, and I think he loves everybody regardless of what label they have."
> "Well, Christianity and being a true believer, you know, I think there's the body of Christ which comes from all the Christian groups around the world, or outside the Christian groups. I think that everybody that loves Christ or knows Christ, whether they're conscious of it or not, they're members of the body of Christ. And I don't think that we're going to see a great sweeping revival that will turn the whole world to Christ at any time."
> "What God is doing today is calling people out of the world for His name. Whether they come from the Muslim world, or the Buddhist world, or the Christian world, or the non-believing world, they are members of the body of Christ because they've been called by God. **They may not even know the name**

of Jesus, but they know in their hearts they need something that they don't have and they turn to the only light they have and **I think they're saved and they're going to be with us in heaven.**"[41]

Can anyone doubt the influence of the famous (neo)evangelist of our time, Billy Graham? How did he come up with "another gospel" so different from Paul's gospel? It can only be through the influence of modern proponents of TC and CT translations, such as the NIV, which remove such important words as *"on me."*

Individuals like Billy Graham are misled and their emotions have clouded their thinking, just like what happened to the Apostle Peter. They place God's love above or in juxtaposition to the reality of a precise Contract with God through Preservation of His Words. The Gospel demands repentance and turning from sin in order to be saved and to avoid judgment. All of these things are part of salvation. This does not mean a person must know all before salvation, but a hunger to know God's will must be present. God's will is God's Contract as delineated in God's Words.

This is the significance of Paul's warnings about *"another gospel"* in Galatians 1:7-9; that is, the Gospel of God is precise and may not be altered by the addition of ANYTHING. Similarly, the Words of God are precise and may not be altered by ANY OTHER WORDS. Otherwise, a person perverts God's grace and mercy as given in a precise Contract. IT IS HIS WILL.

Unbelievers, such as apostates and heretics, who are *"condemned already,"* have no qualms about destroying or corrupting the Words of God (Jn. 3:17-18). The alterations they make are subtle.

---

[41] These quotes have been well documented in many places. This came from http://vintagechristianity.wordpress.com/2007/07/24/billy-graham-denies-the-gospel/

Unless a person is diligent and studies the changes carefully, the altered message that results from the revision will be missed. The new Words introduced by man will not carry the same message or the same impact as *"the **words** of eternal life"* (Jn. 6:68).

Destruction of the Words of God

On many occasions in history, an attempt has been made to destroy the Words as opposed to altering them. For example, God gave specific Words to Jeremiah that Baruck, his amanuensis, recorded. The scroll was carried to King Jehoiakim, king of Judah, and read by Jehudi.

> *"And it came to pass, that when Jehudi had read three or four leaves, he (King Jehoiakim) cut it with the penknife, and cast it into the fire that was on the hearth, until all the roll was consumed in the fire that was on the hearth."* Jeremiah 36:23 (HDW, my addition).

The King's punishment was outlined in verse thirty.

> *"Therefore thus saith the LORD of Jehoiakim king of Judah; He shall have none to sit upon the throne of David: and his dead body shall be cast out in the day to the heat, and in the night to the frost."* Jeremiah 36:30

Who is not aware of the various governments in history who have destroyed the records and the Bible of God's people? This synopsis will not deal with quotes or examples except to mention the Roman Empire's persecution of Christians as well as the Roman Catholic Church's attacks for many centuries. Their aggressions toward

Donatists, Novatians, Waldensians, Huguenots, Albigensians, Petrobrussians, and many others, is notorious.

How much worse will the punishment be in *"the day of the Lord"* for those who have subtly altered God's "rule" or canon (2 Cor. 10:13, Phil. 3:16) and destroyed the people of God? Never forget, man is living currently in the Age of Grace when failure of a believer is forgiven by repentance. Often, when repentance does not occur, punishment is delayed for a season. Now that's grace.

> *"Because sentence against an evil work is not executed speedily, therefore the heart of the sons of men is fully set in them to do evil." (Ecclesiastes 8:11)*

I fear that many men carry on with their obvious contrary position thinking that since judgment has not come upon them that they are on the right track. Think again!

The Words of God were given to man by the Holy Spirit to be recorded. The denial of their origin, purpose, importance, and message is analogous to blasphemy of the Holy Spirit. God help those who have handled the Words of God carelessly. God, who inspired the Scripture, has throughout the years protected His Words from the attacks of evil men so as to preserve them pure, infallible, and inerrant. He warns man repeatedly either by exalting His Words or by cautioning evil men to be VERY aware of what they are doing. Let us examine a few verses that exemplify the honour God attributes to His Words and to Himself, the source of the Words. God declares 164 times in the Scripture these words: *"I am the Lord."* Furthermore, He proclaims:

> *"Thus saith the LORD, thy redeemer, and he that formed thee from the womb,* **I am the LORD** *that maketh all things; that stretcheth forth the heavens alone; that spreadeth abroad the earth by myself;"*

*Isaiah 44:24 "That they may know from the rising of the sun, and from the west, that there is none beside me. **I am the LORD**, and there is none else. Isaiah 45:6*

In addition, Jesus, who declared He was God, said this of Himself ten (10) times: *"I am he,"* and He says:

*"I said therefore unto you, that ye shall die in your sins: for if ye believe not that **I am he**, ye shall die in your sins." John 8:24*

"I am He" (or in other Words, God Himself) declares in His answer to His archenemy:

*"But he answered and said, **It is written,** Man shall not live by bread alone, but by **every word that proceedeth out of the mouth of God**." Matthew 4:4*

It doesn't get any clearer. Furthermore, Jesus said unto His disciples:

"Heaven and earth shall pass away, but my words shall not pass away."[42] Matthew 24:35 (cf. Mk. 13:31, Lk. 21:33).

Do you believe God would abandon His Words, giving them to man, to be reconstructed? King David, speaking the Words from the Holy Spirit said:

---

[42] This verse contains the strongest negative in the Greek language, "ou me." The verse is repeated exactly two more times in Mk. 13:31 and Lk. 21:33, making it the same statement in Scripture **three times**, which is a significant number in the Bible.

*"I will worship toward thy holy temple, and praise thy name for thy lovingkindness and for thy truth: **for thou hast magnified thy word above all thy name.**"* Psalms 138:2 (HDW, my emphasis).

In addition, consider the following:

"Thus speaketh the LORD God of Israel, saying, Write thee all the words that I have spoken unto thee in a book." Jeremiah 30:2 "The grass withereth, the flower fadeth: but the word of our God shall stand for ever." Isaiah 40:8 "Being born again, not of corruptible seed, but of incorruptible, by the word of God, which liveth and abideth for ever. For all flesh is as grass, and all the glory of man as the flower of grass. The grass withereth, and the flower thereof falleth away: But the word of the Lord endureth for ever. And this is the word which by the gospel is preached unto you." 1 Peter 1:23-25 "And I have put my words in thy mouth, and I have covered thee in the shadow of mine hand, that I may plant the heavens, and lay the foundations of the earth, and say unto Zion, Thou art my people." Isaiah 51:16

"Then the LORD put forth his hand, and touched my mouth. And the LORD said unto me, Behold, I have put my words in thy mouth." Jeremiah 1:9

So shall my word be that goeth forth out of my mouth: it shall not return unto me void, but it shall accomplish that which I please, and it shall prosper in the thing whereto I sent it. Isaiah 55:11 "For all those things hath mine hand made, and all those things have been, saith the LORD: but to this man will I look, even to him that is poor and of a contrite spirit, and trembleth at my word." Isaiah 66:2

"The ungodly are not so: but are like the chaff which the wind driveth away." Psalms 1:4 "Therefore as the fire devoureth the stubble, and the flame consumeth the chaff, so their root shall be as rottenness, and their blossom shall go up as dust: because they have cast away the law of the LORD of hosts, and despised the word of the Holy One of Israel." Isaiah 5:24 "The prophet that hath a dream, let him tell a dream; and he

that hath my word, let him speak my word faithfully. What is the chaff to the wheat? saith the LORD." Jeremiah 23:28 *The instruments also of the churl are evil: he deviseth wicked devices to destroy the poor with lying words, even when the needy speaketh right."* Isaiah 32:7 *"In transgressing and lying against the LORD, and departing away from our God, speaking oppression and revolt, conceiving and uttering from the heart words of falsehood."* Isaiah 59:13 *"To whom shall I speak, and give warning, that they may hear? behold, their ear is uncircumcised, and they cannot hearken: behold, the word of the LORD is unto them a reproach; they have no delight in it."* Jeremiah 6:10

*"Behold, ye trust in **lying words**, that cannot profit."* Jeremiah 7:8 *"The wise men are ashamed, they are dismayed and taken: lo, they have rejected the word of the LORD; and what wisdom is in them?"* Jeremiah 8:9 *"Hear ye the word which the LORD speaketh unto you, ..."* Jeremiah 10:1 *"Then the LORD said unto me, Proclaim all these words ..., saying, Hear ye the words of this covenant, and do them. Yet they obeyed not, nor inclined their ear, but walked every one in the imagination of their evil heart: therefore I will bring upon them all the words of this covenant, which I commanded them to do; but they did them not."* Jeremiah 11:8 *"This evil people, which refuse to hear my words, which walk in the imagination of their heart, and walk after other gods, to serve them, and to worship them, shall even be as this girdle, which is good for nothing."* Jeremiah 13:10 *"...they have hardened their necks, that they might not hear my words."* Jeremiah 19:15 *"O earth, earth, earth, hear the word of the LORD."* Jeremiah 22:29 *"Thus saith the LORD of hosts, Hearken not unto the words of the prophets that prophesy unto you: they make you vain: they speak a vision of their own heart, and not out of the mouth of the LORD."* Jeremiah 23:16 *"For who hath stood in the counsel of the LORD, and hath perceived and heard his word? who hath marked his word, and heard it?"* Jeremiah 23:18 *"But if they had stood in my counsel, and had caused my people to hear my words, then they should have turned them*

from their evil way, and from the evil of their doings." Jeremiah 23:22 *"Am I a God at hand, saith the LORD, and not a God afar off?"* Jeremiah 23:23 *"Is not my word like as a fire? saith the LORD; and like a hammer that breaketh the rock in pieces?"* Jeremiah 23:29 *"And the burden of the LORD shall ye mention no more: for every man's word shall be his burden; for ye have perverted the words of the living God, of the LORD of hosts our God."* Jeremiah 23:36 *"Therefore thus saith the LORD of hosts; Because ye have not heard my words,"* Jeremiah 25:8

"Therefore prophesy thou against them all these words, and say unto them, The LORD shall roar from on high, and utter his voice from his holy habitation; he shall mightily roar upon his habitation; he shall give a shout, as they that tread the grapes, against all the inhabitants of the earth." Jeremiah 25:30 "Because they have not hearkened to my words, saith the LORD, which I sent unto them by my servants the prophets, rising up early and sending them; but ye would not hear, saith the LORD." Jeremiah 29:19

CHAPTER 2

THE MODERN CRITICAL TEXT

"The simple believeth every word: but the prudent man looketh well to his going." Proverbs 14:15

Two Types of Critical Texts

A *'modern'* Critical Text (CT) of the Bible[43] is any text that is determined by the 'new' discipline of textual criticism. One type is sometimes called the eclectic text because of the method by which it was constructed from an assortment of a handful of corrupted texts. A second type of Critical Text is the Majority Text that aims to establish the original Greek text by a 'critical examination' of most of the manuscripts without any favoritism. For many reasons, this will never be accomplished because of the difficulty, cost, training, time, dispersion of the texts to many countries' museums, fragility of the texts, and similar.

The non-textual critic simply recognizes and *receives* the Words of God by faith. It is not a non-intellectual or unreasoned

---

[43] "Critical Text of the Greek New Testament determined through textual criticism. There are two main New Testament text traditions today (with various subtypes); the critical text, based on the text types which have the oldest copies available today, and the Majority Text, which gives priority to the text types with the largest number of text copies available today. The critical text is also known as the eclectic text. The main critical text of the New Testament used today is the Nestle-Aland text, which appears in another edition as the UBS text." www.geocities.com/bible_translation/glossco.htm

approach as textual critics charge; it requires significant knowledge, wisdom, prudence, and understanding.

The Seeds of Modern Textual Criticism

The seeds of the *modern* textual critic's tenets can be indentified in Scripture (q.v.). The instigator was Satan as he purposefully questioned and changed the Words of God. The underlying intellectual and emotional basis, which would allow this tragedy, begins with (1) contempt of God and (2) disregard of His clear, pure, easily understood "Proclamations" (Mat. 4:4, 24:35, Mk. 13:31, Lk. 21:33, 1 Pe. 1:23-25, Psa. 12:6-7, etc. etc.).

The Greek Philosophers

The validity of these two factors can be demonstrated in the writings of the three very important Greek philosophers, Socrates (471-399 BC), Plato (427-347 BC), and Aristotle (384-322 BC), who lived before the first coming of the Lord Jesus Christ. For example, the homosexual, Plato, taught principles to his students that are clearly against Old Testament precepts, such as the following:

1. Infanticide, which is killing a child who is deformed or impaired such as a child with trisomy or Down's syndrome (mongolism).
2. Socialism.
3. Selective breeding.
4. Kidnapping of children from their parents for a 20 year period of state-controlled values clarification.
5. Distrust of the physical world.

Dr. James Sightler, M.D., said:

"Plato was a despiser of the God of Moses and tried to remake God in the image of Plato. He taught a counterfeit trinity: first, the absolute pure being incomprehensible to man's mind; second, the Logos or Universal or Divine Nous; and third, the Soul of the World which proceeded from the Logos."[44]

The Logos in Plato's writings was the corruption of the preincarnate Lord Jesus Christ (Gen. 16:7). In the Old Testament, He was the *"angel of the Lord."* The term occurs 68 times in the OT. Plato's Logos was a *created* being that *created* the "soul of the world," a perversion of the Holy Spirit (Psa. 51:11, Isa. 63:10, etc.). These human philosophical opinions can be identified in three significant theological divisions among cults that are opposed to the precepts in the Bible.

1. The first is Arianism, which taught that Jesus was a created being, but a God.

2. The second is Socinianism, which went even further than Arianism by teaching that Jesus was *not* God.

3. The third, Sabellianism or Unitarianism, taught that there was no Trinity, and that Jesus was simply another manifestation of one God who was also the Father and the Spirit, but in different modes. This is often called modalism.

Many Gnostic cults did not believe that Jesus was God in the flesh. One of their 'ideas' was that material substances were evil, so God could not possibly be walking the earth in a fleshly body. The Socinians were probably responsible for the removal of the word, Jesus, or Christ, from many verses in the Bible because of their claim that Jesus could not possibly be God.

---

[44] James H. Sightler, M.D., *Tabernacle Essays on Bible Translation* (Sightler Publications, Greenville, SC, 1993) 6.

What emanates from and undergirds the cults is a false theological assertion that supports most of their reasoning. It is the unanimous assertion and concerted opinion that 'good ideas' (knowledge) lead man to perform 'good deeds' or 'good works,' thus pleasing the gods. Subsequently, knowledge of divine 'things' produces "works" or good deeds that lead to salvation and ultimately to happiness, virtue, and approval of the gods. The preceding is the outcome or progression of the philosophy of "the unholy Greek triumvirate." It is said of Aristotle, the student of Plato:

> "Aristotle describes virtue or excellence as "a characteristic involving choice, consisting in observing the mean relative to us, a mean which is determined by a rational principle; such as a person of practical wisdom would use [the mean determined by the rational principle to determine [virtue]" (*Nicomachean Ethics* II.6). ("Practical wisdom" is "a truthful characteristic of acting with reason in matters good and bad for humans," VI.5.)" [and] **Virtue or excellence is not simply doing the "right thing," whatever that is. To be virtuous, an action must be done at the right time, for the right reason (namely, for the sake of the beautiful or noble or good, toward the right people, and in the right manner** (II.6).[45]

These thoughts undergird the modern theories of situational ethics and relativism. Obviously, the "right thing(s)" are God's precepts, commandments, judgments, and testaments, which are clearly taught in the OT and were readily available during the lives of

---

[45] http://74.125.45.104/search?q=cache:qkxYBPYEjhMJ:www.gmu.edu/ courses/phil/ancient/ollispa.ppt+Plato+and+good+deeds&hl=en&ct=clnk&cd =7&gl=us. It is significant that Lk. 2:14, which reads: *"Glory to God in the highest and on earth peace, good will toward men"* (KJB) is changed in many new versions to reflect Greek philosophy and reads, *"Glory to God in the highest, and on earth peace to men on whom his favor rests."(NIV)*.

the unholy triumvirate of Socrates, Plato, and Aristotle (Gen. 15:6, Gal. 3:6, Rom. 4:3, etc.). Many copies of the Scriptures were produced for leaders in the nation Israel and available to others. The unholy triumvirate rejected them. Aristotle's statement is truly a political statement that leads to the modern world's definition of tolerance.[46] The ultimate outcome of such depraved thinking leads to false liberty (rather than liberty in Christ, Gal. 2:4, 5:1) and results in many evils such as fornication, adultery, homosexualism, etc. (Gal. 5:19-21).

Greek philosophy is pragmatism at its worst. Early in the apostolic era, the Apostle Paul clearly warned believers about man's philosophy and salvation by works. It deceives. He said:

> "Beware lest any man spoil you through philosophy and vain deceit, after the tradition of men, after the rudiments of the world, and not after Christ." Colossians 2:8 (HDW, Colossians was written about 61 AD). "And if by grace, then is it no more of works: otherwise grace is no more grace. But if it be of works, then is it no more grace: otherwise work is no more work." Romans 11:6

Scriptural Warnings
About Textual Critics and Criticism

Many of the writings in the NT were for the purpose of correcting these ubiquitous fallacious human philosophies, positions, and doctrines, (cf. John1:1ff, 1 Jn. 1:1ff, Galatians, Colossians, etc.). The smooth words of charismatic elocutionists or skillful writers mislead

---

[46] No rebuking, reproving, or public disagreement with anyone's doctrines, beliefs, statements, etc., only political correctness in contrast to 2 Tim. 4:2-4. Previously, tolerance was the right to express one's views without violence; this has been squelched in modern society because of the rejection of Christian beliefs and the agenda of anti-Christian groups.

many. Hoodwinked individuals will change the Words 'received' from a Holy God to make them correspond to their beliefs. This is exactly what was happening in the apostolic era to the Apostle Paul. Undoubtedly, it was recorded for our learning. Paul said:

> *"That ye be not soon shaken in mind, or be troubled, neither by spirit, nor by word, nor by letter **as from us**, as that the day of Christ is at hand." 2 Thessalonians 2:2 (HDW, my emphasis)*

Men were sending out letters, which corrupted the Words of God, as if they were from the Apostle himself. Consequently, many false 'letters' or 'books' have been published under the pseudonyms of the apostles or as pseudoepigraphal writings, such as *The Book of Jubilees, The Gospel of Peter, The Gospel of Barnabas, The Shepherd of Hermas, The Gospel of Judas,* and *The Gospel of Thomas.* Without a doubt, they contain the seeds of Arianism, Socinianism, and Unitarianism. The seeds in these three heretical philosophies, as well as in other Gnostic cults, promote "knowledge," "insight," and "mysticism," which leads to works as the key to salvation. Furthermore, many flatly deny the deity, virgin birth, bodily resurrection, and ascension of the Lord Jesus Christ.

These same principles are evident in the writings of the primary men associated with the tenets of modern textual criticism, Brooke Foss Westcott (1825-1903) and F. H. A. Hort (1828-1892) **(q.v.)**. The principles were developed over several hundred years, but culminated with Westcott and Hort.[47] They believed their views would

---

[47] Pastor D. A. Waite, *The Heresies of Westcott and Hort As Seen In Their Own Writings* (Bible For Today, Collingswood, NJ, 1979) And see *Westcott's Denial of Christ's Bodily Resurrection* by the same author, BFT #1131.

lead them to "the most likely form of the original text."[48] They attempted to judge the differences in texts by using their tenets to arrive at which variants in copies of texts or manuscripts (MSS) are the "original readings" even though they did not have the original apostolic manuscripts. Therefore, the tenets that they used become a very important consideration (q.v.). Do these tenets generate a valid system to use?

Influential Men In the History of Corruption

Before we address this question, let us first explore other and earlier influential men before Westcott and Hort in the history of corruption of the Words of God 'received' through the nation Israel and the churches (Lk. 6:48ff, Jn. 17:8, Rom. 3:1-2, 1 Co. 3:11, Eph. 2:20, 1 Tim. 3:15). It is important to mention circumstantial evidence at this point.

> "Circumstantial evidence is best explained by saying what it is not — it is not direct evidence from a witness who saw or heard something. Circumstantial evidence is a fact that can be used to infer another fact. Indirect evidence that implies something occurred but doesn't directly prove it; proof of one or more facts from which one can find another fact; proof of a chain of facts and circumstances indicating that the person is either guilty or not guilty."[49]

Philo Judaeus

Although we cannot prove the following relationships and influences, the circumstantial evidence is HIGH. That is the reason for

---

[48] www.geocities.com/bible_translation/glossco.htm "Critical Apparatus."
[49] http://www.lectlaw.com/def/c342.htm

the warnings in Scripture concerning the doctrine of separation and its importance (Rom. 16:17-18, and MANY other places in Scripture). Having said that, the next person to consider in history is the Alexandrian Jew by the name of **Philo Judaeus** (c. 20 BC – 50 AD). As contact is important in the spread of disease, so it is in the spread of heresy and apostasy.

Philo Judaeus was writing literature that amalgamated Jewish sacred Scripture (the Old Testament) with the ideas of Plato. Later, during the Reformation, this practice would be called "Scholasticism." He was a member of a wealthy Jewish family in Alexandria, Egypt and was well educated in Greek schools. Philo's writings—particularly his commentaries on the Scriptures—influenced the early church. Here are some of the problems with Philo:

1. He was known for use of allegory. He believed literal interpretation was proper for the average scholar, but for the enlightened ones such as himself, he advocated an allegorical interpretation. His harmonization of Judaism and Platonism gave rise to Neo-Platonism.

2. The essences of his teachings were:

> a. The Logos or Reason created the universe, not God or the Absolute.

> b. The Logos was assisted by a number of intermediate beings known as the Pleroma.

> c. The account of the creation in Genesis was a myth, and only reflected how the creation was conceived in the mind of God.

Founder of the Alexandrian School, Pantaenus

Philo's teachings influenced **Pantaenus** (c. 181 A.D.) who founded and taught theologians at the infamous Catechetical School at Alexandria, Egypt. Pantaenus was noted for being one of the "deepest Gnostics." One of his students was **Clement of Alexandria** (A.D. 150-217), a "church father" who subsequently educated Origen (182-251 A.D.) and who was honored to be called a Gnostic. Clement believed Plato was inspired because his writings contained the truth. His great mission was to show the bridge between the Gospel and the wisdom of Gentiles, and to show how a believer could rise to the position of a true Gnostic.[50]

Origen

Origen (182-251 AD), a student of Clement of Alexandria, was probably the worst heretic and perverter of Scripture in history.

1. He sided with Arius in his teachings that Jesus was a created being, who was not eternally generated.[51]

2. He denied a literal Hell.

3. He denied a physical resurrection.

4. He also believed in the preexistence of the human soul.

5. He believed in regeneration by baptism.

6. He believed in infant sprinkling.

7. He taught transubstantiation.

8. He alleged that Satan was paid a ransom by Christ's death, which allowed a "mystical kiss", whatever that means.

---

[50] Grady, op. cit., p. 82 *(Final Authority)*.
[51] James H. Sightler, M.D., *Tabernacle Essays on Bible Translation;* p. 6-7.

9. He allegorically dismissed the Passover, Jesus' wilderness temptation, and the purging of Herod's temple.

10. He accepted the Apocrypha and attributed the formulation of his allegorical system to the *"Shepherd of Hermas."*

11. He had very little faith in the Scriptures. He said:

> "I do not condemn them (authors of Scripture) if they even sometimes dealt freely with things which to the eye of history happened differently, and changed them so as to subserve the mystical aims they had in view; so as to speak of a thing which happened in a certain place, as if it happened in another, or what took place at a certain time, as if it had taken place at another time, and to introduce into what was spoken in a certain way some changes of their own. They proposed to speak the truth where it was possible both materially and spiritually, and where this was not possible it was their intention to prefer the spiritual to the material. The spiritual truth was often preserved, as one might say, in the material falsehood."[52]

In spite of beliefs like these, Origin was venerated by many scholars throughout history and is respected even today.

12. His mental faculties may have also been affected by his self-mutilation, the act of castrating himself out of a misinterpretation of Matthew 19:12: ***For there are some eunuchs, which were so born from their mother's womb: and there are some eunuchs, which were made eunuchs of men: and there be eunuchs, which have made themselves eunuchs for the kingdom of heaven's sake. He that is able to receive it, let him receive it.*** If he had only read Deuteronomy 23:1 *He that is wounded in the stones, or hath his privy member cut off, shall not*

---

[52] Dr. William P. Grady, Th.D., Ph.D., *Final Authority* (Grady Publications, Knoxville, TN, 1993) p. 94.

enter into the congregation of the LORD, *he could have saved himself a lot of pain.*[53]

Whether Origen actually changed the manuscripts of the Scriptures is not known for sure, but his prolific writings quote over 30,000 references to the Words that may have been wrongly quoted in order to "mesh" them with his scheme of belief. However, it is impossible to establish which manuscripts he used; the same being true of a disciple and follower of Origen, **Eusebius** (260-341 A.D.). Wilbur Pickering, quoting Zundz's *"The Text,"* says:

> "The insuperable difficulties opposing the establishment of "the" New Testament text of Origen and Eusebius are well known to all who have attempted it...Leaving aside the common difficulties imposed by the uncertainties of the transmission, the incompleteness of the material, and the **frequent freedom of quotation**, there is the incontestable fact that these two Fathers are frequently at variance; that each of them quotes the same passage differently in different writings; and that sometimes they do so even within the compass of one and the same work...Wherever one and the same passage is extant in more than one quotation by Origen or Eusebius, variation between them is the rule rather than the exception."[54]

Eusebius And Pamphilus

Origen was finally run out of Alexandria because of heresy and settled in Caesarea, a city on the edge of Judea and Syria. Here he established another school and library. After his death, **Pamphilus** (240-309 A.D.), his pupil, continued to catalogue his extensive

---

[53] Grady, op. cit, p. 90 *(Final Authority)*.
[54] Wilbur N. Pickering, *The Identity Of The New Testament Text* (Thomas Nelson Publisher, Nashville, TN, 1980) p. 64.

writings. The library he established was the repository of Origen's famous Hexapla. The Hexapla of Origen contained six versions of the Bible in Hebrew and Greek, side by side for comparison, and it is suspected of being the source of the very important Septuagint manuscripts, Aleph and B. The new head of Origen's Palestinian school after his death was his trusted student, Pamphilus, who became the mentor and teacher, amazingly, of Eusebius, the Bishop of Caesarea.

> After the emperor of Rome, Constantine, was "converted" to Christianity on the battlefield in the early 4th century by a vision of a cross, he appointed Eusebius to produce the Bible for the empire. Incidentally, the same library Eusebius used, became the source of Jerome's research that produced the Latin Vulgate. Eusebius produced the very important New Testament codices, Vaticanus, also known as B, and Siniaticus, also known as Aleph.[55] When Constantine ordered 50 new "Bibles" made by Eusebius (now named Eusebius Pamphili after his mentor), he went to Pamphilus' Caesarean library and worked with numerous copyists to fill the order. Dean John William Burgon (1813-1888 A.D.), one of the world's great textual scholars, surmises, "Constantine applied to Eusebius for fifty handsome copies amongst which it is not improbable that the manuscripts...B and Aleph were to be actually found." And that such an opinion was not restricted to Majority advocates (this will be explained later) is evidenced by Constantine Tischendorf's (1815-1874) (another textual scholar) euphoric speculation that "Is it possible that this Bible (Aleph) could be one of the 50 copies which Emperor Constantine ordered Eusebius to place in Constantinople, his new capital?"[56]

---

[55] Ibid. p. 7 (*Final Authority*).
[56] Ibid. p. 110 (*Final Authority*).

The old saying comes to mind, "Where there is smoke, there is fire." There are many other reasons Burgon and Tischendorf concluded that Eusebius made the codices, Aleph and B. We will deal with those facts later in the section on manuscripts.

Jerome, The Latin Vulgate, And Old Latin MSS

Most scholars believe that Jerome, who constructed the Latin Vulgate, used Alexandrian-type manuscripts. Through the centuries, the Latin Vulgate-type MSS have presented many problems, which are too extensive to explore in this brief work. Popes and Catholic scholars constantly manipulated the text. The Latin Vulgate MSS have had a significant influence on the reconstruction of the modern Critical Text.

Following the above very important persons (VIP's), Plato, Origen, and Eusebius, we will skip to the 19th century and the alleged "rediscovery" of the Vaticanus (B) and Sinaiticus (Aleph) codices (animal hides used for writing made into "books"). This does not mean that ongoing significant corruptions of texts was not taking place during the centuries between, or that Satan was not using his instruments to try to destroy confidence in the Bible during this time. It is well-known that during the Middles Ages, Rome, through the Roman Catholic Church, tried to stamp out every MSS and religious group that came against their text and their church. It is also well-known that the Old Latin MSS, which were used by the Waldensians, Albigensians, Novatians, and others, were translations much closer to the TR/TT. The Old Latin continued to be preferred over Rome's Latin text for about 1000 years. Finally, at the Council of Trent (began in 1545), Rome:

1. Declared its authority over the text of Scripture, saying "tradition" was of equal authority.

2. Denied the teachings of the Reformation.

3. Decreed justification was not by faith alone in the shed blood of Jesus Christ, and many other abominations.

Would you want this church with its Society of Jesus (Jesuits) that enforced domination over governments by murder, lies, and subterfuge to preserve, guard, watch over, and protect the *"jots and tittles"* of the Words of God? In summary, there was extreme violent opposition to the "plain" Christians and their text during the Dark Ages.

Influence of Aleph and B Codices on Men

Returning to our discussion of the Aleph and Vaticanus (B) MSS, many significant scholars believe that they were lost for about 1500 years. However, that is not the case. They were very likely used by Jerome or, at least, he used local-type MSS that came from Alexandria where B and Aleph originated. Bruce Metzger, the Princeton text scholar, who proved his apostasy by publishing the Readers Digest Condensed Bible, admits Jerome used Alexandrian-type MSS.

Many authorities believe the manuscripts (codices), Aleph and B, survived because of their rejection by the vulgate (common) church, as well as the Roman Catholic Church, because they were **SO** corrupted, (i.e. they were put in storage and not used) or perhaps, because of their lack of use by the new church of the empire, the Roman Catholic Church, which preferred their ever-changing Latin Vulgate text. Whatever the case, Jerome (A.D. 347-419) used local Alexandrian text-types in the preparation of the Latin Vulgate (A.D. 405). The Roman Catholic Church eventually declared the Latin Vulgate as their official Bible, and anyone translating the Bible into another language was persecuted, placed in prison, or killed.[57] The Roman church did not want the Bible in the hands of laymen. They recognized that Truth sets men free. They wanted the masses under their heavy hand for their manipulation for "mammon."

Westcott, Hort, And Tischendorf

Several men enthusiastically embraced the "rediscovered" B and Aleph codices in the 19th century. They idolized the manuscripts. The principal players were: 1. **Brook Foss Westcott** (1828-1903) 2. **Fenton John Hort** (1828-1892) and 3. **Constantine Tischendorf** (1815-1874).

Development of "Rationalistic" Textual Criticism

Tischendorf was a German textual scholar strongly influenced by the rationalistic thinking of his age. The development of rationalistic textual criticism is interesting. In the early Reformation period, the invention of the printing press by Gutenberg in 1452 allowed men such as Erasmus (1466-1536), Stephanus (1503-1559), Calvin (1509-1564) and Beza (1519-1605) to begin listing differences in manuscripts in the margins. However, they accepted the Greek Traditional and Hebrew Masoretic texts, which were used by the majority of churches in Syria, Italy, France, Spain, and Germany. **There were few differences in the texts.** What differences were present in the original-language texts, they considered "accidental"

---

[57] See *Wycliffe Controversies* by this author available on Amazon. Type in the title, not the authors name. H. D. Williams, *Wycliffe Controversies* (The Old Paths Publications, Cleveland, GA, 2008).

differences. They (Erasmus et al.) approached the text in a more theological way, believing that God preserved the text. They did not consider that emendations (changes) were made in the 'received' text on purpose. They only tried to establish the correct readings. They were not enthusiastic about the Latin Vulgate of Jerome and the Roman Church[58] or depraved MSS Aleph and B, which had been obviously defaced by multiple scribes.

Early Influences

Early in the age of rationalism, **Hugo Grotius** (1583-1645), a famous theologian and statesman from Holland, began making speculative changes in the text like one might make with a secular book. Another Dutchman, **Stephen Courcelles** (c. 1658), continued this trend, which alarmed "the faithful" and drew new attention to the New Testament Text.

Richard Simon, a French priest, was also involved early on. The Catholic Encyclopedia reports:

> "A French priest, Richard Simon (1638-1712), was the first who subjected the general questions concerning the Bible to a treatment which was at once comprehensive in scope and scientific in method. Simon is the forerunner of modern Biblical criticism...The use of internal evidence by which Simon arrived at it entitles him to be called the father of Biblical criticism."

John Fell in 1675 at Oxford suggested ways that the scribes may have changed the text and in 1711 **Gerhard von Maestricht**

---

[58] Erasmus of Rotterdam, *Praise of Folly and Letter to Maarten Van Dorp* (Penguin Books, reprint 1993, original 1515). This is a parody about Erasmus' contempt for the Roman Catholic Church and their priests.

published a list of 43 rules to deal with those alleged mistakes. Subsequently, attention was shifted away from the original Apostolic authors to inattentive scribes according to Dr. Edward F. Hills, one of history's finest textual critics.[59] Hills was a Phi Beta Kappa graduate of Yale University. He earned degrees from Westminster Theological Seminary and Columbia Theological Seminary. He completed his Th.D. at Harvard in textual criticism.

Development of a "New" Greek Text

Shortly after Fell and von Maestricht, searches began for the "oldest" manuscripts in order to establish a completely 'new' (altered) Greek text that would replace the traditional Greek text, which had always been accepted by the dissenters from the Roman Catholic Church as the Words of God.

A Cambridge scholar by the name of **Richard Bently** (1662-1742) planned a "thoroughly naturalistic method" of textual criticism in the hope of reproducing the N.T. Greek text that was supposedly available at the time of the Council of Nicea (325 A.D.) and supposedly subsequently lost.[60] Adding to the parameters of textual criticism was **J. A. Bengel** (1687-1752). He advocated that the hardest reading should be preferred over the easiest reading. This caused quite a stir in Germany among the orthodox Christians. I suppose orthodox churches were insulted by the implication that the saints could not understand the more difficult readings; and so the scribes had chosen an easier reading and therefore corrupted the manuscripts.

---

[59] Edward F. Hills, *The King James Version Defended* (Christian research Press, Des Moines, Iowa, 4th edition, reprint, 1993) pp. 62-63.
[60] Ibid. p. 64 (Hills, *The King James Version Defended*).

Incidentally, this same attitude persists today among "scholars." While preparing this work, the author encountered many disparaging remarks concerning Saints who have investigated the two paths that the texts of the New Testament have taken. Here is an example found on the "Advent.com" internet site:

> "One must be careful in assessing people who ....are *not* textual critics, and do not engage in textual criticism. Anyone...who claims providential preservation or some kind of divine sanction for a particular text, is not and cannot be a textual critic. It is unfortunate that these non-critics have infected the arguments about the... text, as their irrational, unreasonable, and uncritical arguments serve only to muddy what should be a reasonable and fruitful debate. It is even more unfortunate that some legitimate critics ... have accepted their rhetoric. This argument, like all critical arguments, must be decided based on evidence and logic, not faith or claims of what "must" be so. The typical argument is "providential preservation" -- the claim that God *must* have preserved the original text in all its purity. But as Harry A. Sturz (who is about as sympathetic to the Byzantine text as anyone can be while not being a pure Byzantine-prioritist) notes:
>> "Hills [the leading exponent of this sort of preservation] fails to show why the sovereign God *must* act in a particular way [Harry A. Sturz, *The Byzantine Text-Type & New Testament Textual Criticism* (1984), p. 42. Italics added.]"[61]

No one can show why God acts in a certain way. His ways are a mystery until revealed (Rom. 16:25). God says:

> *"For my thoughts are not your thoughts, neither are your ways my ways, saith the* LORD*" (Isaiah 55:8)*

---

[61] Internet site: Advent.com.

If you read the above closely, you immediately realize that Harry Sturz must have a limited concept of **the priesthood of believers** guided by the Holy Spirit and needs to be reminded of 1 Peter 2:9:

> *But ye are a chosen generation, a royal priesthood, an holy nation, a peculiar people; that ye should shew forth the praises of him who hath called you out of darkness into his marvellous light: and Col. 2:8 Beware lest any man spoil you through philosophy and vain deceit, after the tradition of men, after the rudiments of the world, and not after Christ.*

Further along in this same article on Advent.com, the same author makes an equally confusing statement that the path of the text preferred by believers in the Textus Receptus "does **not** show the sort of massive inferiority" that is implied by others in the textual debate. Perhaps he is now trying to sooth roughed-up feathers. I wonder if there is anything ecumenical in his statement?

Surely the attitude of J.A. Bengel must have been as confusing and condescending to the orthodox Saints in Bengel's day as the above author is today. No wonder the German Saints rose up in disdain.

Sowing Seeds of Doubt

The path to Westcott and Hort's tenets continued, however, with the encouragement of a Prussian philosopher king, **Frederick II**, who ruled 46 years (1740-1786). Cynicism toward the Biblical texts progressed and **Johann Semler** (1725-1795) maintained the concept that the Scriptures contained only:

> "Jewish conceptions of merely local and temporal value which it was the task of scientific exegesis to point out."[62]

He also believed the manuscripts had been corrupted by the Scribes with their own additions, subtractions, and changes.

A student of Semler, **J. J. Griesbach** (1745-1812) was so infected with Semler's thinking that he believed the New Testament was contaminated by more glosses, interpolations and additions than any other manuscript. He further added the rule, that:

> "The most suspicious reading of all is the one that yields a sense favorable to the nourishment of piety (especially monastic piety)"[63].

In other words if the reading seems "holy" or orthodox, disregard it.

> "Griesbach's skepticism was shared by J. L. Hug (1765-1846), who in 1808 advanced the theory that in the 2nd century the New Testament text had become deeply degenerate and corrupt and that all extant New Testament tests were merely editorial revisions of the corrupted text. And **Carl Lachmann** (1793-1846) continued in this same skeptical vein. He believed that from the extant manuscripts it was not possible to construct a text which would reach any farther back than the 4th century. To bridge the gap between this reconstruction 4th century text and the original text, Lachmann proposed to resort **to conjectural emendation** [HDW, adding what he conjectured was right,]. In 1831 he published an edition of the Greek New Testament which reflected his views."[64]

---

[62] Hills Th.D., Edward F.; *The King James Version Defended;* p. 65
[63] Ibid. 65
[64] Ibid. 65.

Other Roman Catholics were involved in spreading the seeds of doubt about Scripture. For example, **Jean Astruc** (1684-1766), a famous French Catholic physician, practiced subjectivism and conjecture when he proposed that Moses used two different names of God and therefore used two different MSS to write Genesis. German theologian **Johann Gottfried Eichorn** (1752-1827) expanded his ideas and declared many books in the NT were spurious, false books. Following him, another Catholic priest of Scottish origin, **Alexander Geddes** (1737-1802), speculated that the Pentateuch and Joshua were put together from fragments. Their ideas were the start of the JEDP (Documentary Theory) of the Pentateuch.

The Pivotal Point

With the above background in mind we finally arrive at a pivotal point in the development of the CT. Subtle influences from an obvious source had led 'scholars' to reject the traditional New Testament text [TR/TT]. They believed it was up to them to restore the text of Scripture. Notice, it was no longer the function of the church to guard and protect the Scriptures; rather, 'scholars' institutions of higher learning would determine the Words.

Prominent people involved in this type of thinking were **Brook Foss Westcott** (1828-1903) and **Fenton John Anthony Hort** (1828-1892). They were professors at Cambridge and, incidentally, were contemporaries of the great men of faith, Charles Haddon Spurgeon (the great preacher), William Booth (founder of the Salvation Army), George Mueller (the great supporter of orphanages and missionaries), and many others. While these men were laboring away in the work of the Kingdom, Westcott and Hort were busily preparing their (not God's) 'New' Greek Text. This Greek text would be prepared from the alleged "rediscovery" of Aleph and B manuscripts. The Vaticanus or B manuscript found in the Vatican would be their favorite. Why they favored these manuscripts, which had thousands of changes and thousands of differences between them and other manuscripts, cannot be understood until their lives and beliefs are examined.

> *"... but unto them that are defiled and unbelieving is nothing pure; but even their mind and conscience is defiled." Titus 1:15*

Were Westcott and Hort Really Heretics?

Often, private letters to friends reveal what one truly believes as opposed to the public professions of a leader, scholar, or teacher. Who could ever forget the revelations on tape of Richard Nixon's involvement in the Watergate scandal?

The private letters of Westcott and Hort have been published by their sons. I have tried to obtain their books, but have been unable to achieve that goal. Therefore, writings and quotes from other authors will have to be utilized. Interestingly, I discovered Dr. Samuel C. Gipp's book, *"An Understandable History of the Bible,"* and in chapter 8 he made this statement:

> "Brooke Foss Westcott (1825-1903) and Fenton John Anthony Hort (1828-1892) have been highly controversial figures in biblical history. On one side, their supporters have heralded them as great men of God, having greatly advanced the search for the original Greek text. On the other side, their opponents have leveled charges of heresy, infidelity, apostasy, and many others, claiming that they are guilty of wreaking great damage on the true text of Scripture. I have no desire to "sling mud" nor a desire to hide facts. I believe it is essential at this time that we

examine what we know about these men and their theories concerning the text of the Bible. <u>I long sought for copies of the books about their lives</u>. These are *The Life and Letters of Brooke Foss Westcott*, by his son, Arthur, and *The Life and Letters of Fenton John Anthony Hort*, written by his son. <u>After literally months of trying</u>, I was able to acquire copies of them both for study. [the author of this work was never able to acquire copies, my addition] Most of the material in this section will be directly from these sources so as to prevent it from being secondhand. We cannot blindly accept the finding of any scholar without investigating what his beliefs are concerning the Bible and its doctrines. **Scholarship alone** makes for an inadequate and dangerous authority, therefore we are forced to scrutinize these men's lives."[65] [my emphasis]

This author could not have said it better. Therefore, I will have to rely on quotes by other writers from those private, personal letters of the two men who did more to shape the "New Greek Text" than any others; Westcott and Hort.

Hort stated that it was **their intention to cast on the world a new text before they were branded as heretics**. Listen to his words:

"I have sort of a craving that our text should be cast upon the world before we deal with matters likely to brand us with suspicion. I mean, a text issued by men who are already known for what will undoubtedly be treated as dangerous heresy will have great difficulty in finding its way to regions which it might otherwise

---

[65] Samuel C. Gipp, Th.D., *An Understandable History of the Bible* (Daystar Publishing, Northfield, Ohio; Second Edition; 2000, ISBN 1-890120-13-8) pp.195-196.

hope to reach and whence it would not be easily banished by subsequent alarms."[66]

Westcott said:

"How certainly I should have been proclaimed a heretic."[67]

Speaking about someone else branded as a heretic, he said:

"If he be condemned, what will become of me?"[68]

By now you are wondering why these men were so alarmed at the possibility of being labeled heretics. The following proclamations will help you to understand. Dr. Hort did not believe in the authority of the Bible. He states:

"Evangelicals seem to me perverted rather then untrue. There are, I fear, still more serious differences between us on the subject of authority, and especially the authority of the Bible."[69]

He also did not accept the infallibility of the Scripture, a fact which he mentioned in several places. One example is:

"But I am not able to go as far as you in asserting the absolute infallibility of a canonical writing."[70]

---

[66] Gail A. Riplinger, *New Age Bible Versions* (AV Publications, Munroe, Ohio 1994; ISBN 0-9635845-0-2) pp.622-623.
[67] Ibid. p. 620 (Riplinger).
[68] Ibid. p. 618 (Riplinger).
[69] Gipp, op cit. p. 201 (*Gipp's Understandable History of the Bible*).
[70] Ibid; p 202.

Inspiration was out of the question for these colleagues. He (Hort) refers to:

> "the common orthodox heresy: inspiration" when referring to the Scriptures."[71]

There are other passages, but one gets the idea that they didn't think much of the Bible they read. As a matter of fact:

> "Dr. Hort says on the eve of his epoch-making project of the 'New' Greek Text: "I had no idea till the last few weeks of the importance of texts, having read so little Greek Testament, and dragged on with the **villainous Textus Receptus ...think of that vile Textus Receptus leaning entirely on late MSS.;** it is a blessing there are such early ones."[72] [This is my comment for greater clarity: The Textus Receptus is the Greek New Testament from which many translations were made including the KJB. Also, remember, as cited and explained previously, "older" manuscripts does not mean "uncorrupted or better".]

Strange Bedfellows

It is also reported that Westcott and Hort had "strange bedfellows." They denied the inspiration and infallibility of the Scriptures but they had no trouble believing Charles Darwin, or the two homosexuals, Socrates and Plato, or the drug-addicted Samuel Taylor Coleridge. Dr. Hort wrote Mr. A. MacMillian saying:

> "You seem to make (Greek) philosophy worthless for those who have received the Christian Revelation. To me, though in a hazy way, it seems full of precious truth, of which I find nothing, and should be very much

---

[71] Riplinger, op. cit., p. 32 (*New Age Bible Versions).*
[72] Grady, op. cit. p. 245 (*Final Authority).*

astonished and perplexed to find anything in revelation."[73]

I presume Dr. Hort meant revelation of Scripture, implying there was more "revelation in Greek philosophy (Plato et al.). Dr. Hort joined "the 'Philosophical Society' and comments:

> "Maurice urged me to give attention to Plato and Aristotle and to make them the **center point** of my reading."[74]

And to John Ellerton he writes:

> "But the book which has most engaged me is Darwin. Whatever may be thought of it, it is a book that one is proud to be contemporary with...My feeling is strong that the theory is unanswerable. If so, it opens up a new period."

To his colleague, B.F. Westcott, he wrote excitedly:

> "Have you read Darwin? How I should like to talk with you about it! In spite of difficulties, I am inclined to think it unanswerable. In any case it is a treat to read such a book."[75]

If anyone reading this leans favorably towards Darwinism, he/she may not realize that this type of thinking points to treating the Scriptures as mythology and as having no authority. As we will discover later in this manuscript, these two men were members of the Broad Church whose doctrine accepted evolution as truth, and believed the Scripture was not the final authority.

---

[73] Gipp, op. cit. p. 204 (*Gipp's Understandable History of the Bible*).
[74] Riplinger, op. cit. p. 618 (*New Age Bible Versions*).
[75] Gipp, p. 203 (*Gipp's Understandable History of the Bible*).

Another favorite bedtime story for Dr. Hort was the writings of Samuel T. Coleridge. Coleridge was addicted to heroin because of rheumatoid arthritis. However, I cannot grant this fact as an excuse for a man who traveled to various countries to study with Eastern gurus, who developed the harmony of Christianity and transcendental philosophy, and:

> "who was responsible, more than any other single individual, for the diffusion of German neology through Cambridge University and thence through the Anglican church. His books, *Biographia Literia, Aids to Reflection, Confessions of an Enquiring Spirit* had a profound effect on Julius Hare, J.F.D. Maurice, and John Sterling. Coleridge and Maurice may be said to be the founders of that section of the church known as the Broad Church or Latitudinarian part, which by 1853 had gained the allegiance of 3500 Anglican priests."[76]

Coleridge wrote the *"Kubla Khan"* and he thought his poems were as inspired as King David's Psalms. Maurice, who was Coleridge's chief disciple and a Unitarian, was also mentioned in the personal letters of Westcott and Hort. Drs. Westcott and Hort were also known as "lovers" of drinks made with alcohol. Their personal letters reflect this fact, and one book accused one of them of a hashish habit. Although the latter cannot be confirmed, it would not be a surprise to learn that it was true.

Ghosts and Goblins

Other interesting "investigations" and interests of Westcott and Hort were their involvement in paranormal occurrences. This is mentioned in their letters, but those who favor Westcott and Hort

---

[76] Sightler, op. cit. p. 12 (*Tabernacle Essays on Bible Translation*).

report that it was just youthful interests. For example, James R. White in his book, *The King James Only Controversy*, says:

> "Westcott's involvement in a club (The Ghostly Society or Guild, my addition) was formed to *investigate* strange occurrences, not engage in devilish activity. Some of Westcott's friends called it the Cock and Bull Club."[77]

With this statement he proceeds to excuse their activities as being the possible activity of any sinful person. Gail Riplinger in her book, "*New Age Versions,*" reports that James Webb, a researcher into the occult reports that the Ghostly Guild was an element in the occult underground. Riplinger reports Webb said:

> "Ghost Society [was] founded by no less a person than Edward White Benson, the future Bishop of Canterbury. As A. C. Benson writes in his father's biography, the Archbishop was always more interested in psychic phenomena than he cared to admit. Two members of the Ghost Club became Bishops [Benson and Westcott] and one a Professor of Divinity [Hort]."[78]

Hort writes of his and Westcott's work to set this apparition association in motion:

> "Westcott, Gorham, C. B. Scott, Benson, Bradshaw, Laud etc. and I have started a society for the investigation of ghosts and all supernatural appearances and effects, being disposed to believe that such things really exist...Westcott is drawing up a schedule of questions."[79]

---

[77] James R. White, *The King James Only Controversy Can You Trust the Modern Translations?* ((Bethany House Publishers, Minneapolis, MN, 1995) p. 245.
[78] Riplinger, op. cit. p. 405 (*New Age Versions*).
[79] Ibid. p. 405 (*New Age Versions*).

In the very same letter Hort chaffs the Bible, extant in his day as the King James Bible from the Greek Textus Receptus, as "Villainous." Again we have only circumstantial evidence, but where there is smoke there is fire. Deut. 18:10-11:

> *"There shall not be found among you any one that maketh his son or his daughter to pass through the fire, or that useth divination, or an observer of times, or an enchanter, or a witch, Or a charmer, or a consulter with familiar spirits, or a wizard, or a necromancer."*

The Broad Church

It is important to point out to the reader that we are making an evaluation of the corruption of the Bible text, much like an physician does in an epidemiological study to determine the source and spread of disease. We must find the source of infection and trace the contacts.

Westcott and Hort were pivotal persons in the change in wording of the 'New' Greek text, which became the basis of the modern Bible versions. They were members of the Broad Church in 19th century England. Below are the doctrines of the liberal Broad Church to which Westcott and Hort belonged. This is a long quote from Dr. James Sightler's work:

> "**First**, the doctrine of original sin was denied and along with it the imputation of Adam's sin to his posterity. Sin was defined as selfishness rather than transgression of God's law or was seen as a negation or failure.
> **Second**, the orthodox satisfaction theory of the atonement was denied and the moral influence theory substituted in its place, or atonement was ignored and incarnation stressed instead. By the satisfaction theory Jesus shed His blood on the cross to satisfy the debt of man's sin, as a propitiation, because God's righteousness is of such magnitude and man's sin so great that nothing else would suffice. But the moral

influence theory says that Christ's death was merely the supreme example of God's love, serving only to move men's hearts toward repentance. Many even claimed that propitiation and vicarious sacrifice were barbaric or immoral. Broad Church theology saw salvation not in what Christ did but in what He was, therefore not in atonement at all but in incarnation. For some, salvation was appropriated by the individual through infant baptism and the Eucharist, so that salvation was a system of gradual reformation administered by the church. But for many other Broad churchmen, for Maurice in particular, the incarnation effected a mystical union of Christ with all men, so that all are saved, and the mission of the church is then simply to tell them so.

Before leaving points one and two we should state that the Platonic system of the Logos as a created being, with all souls that will ever be preexisting in the Logos, is driven by the idea of incarnation; that is, Transcendentalism, the Broad Church, and the Catholic Church, all of which incorporated Platonic ideas to greater or lesser degree, have always stressed incarnation and downplayed atonement. On the other hand the Biblical view of man as a fallen, sinful creature, alien from God, is driven by the idea of redemption, and so in this system propitiatory atonement is the primary doctrine and incarnation is correctly limited to Jesus alone for the purpose of atonement.

It is significant that Westcott again in his essay on Origen notes that Origen's writings have no teaching on justification and no theory of atonement. Westcott in this essay clearly sides with Origen as against Augustine, who did believe in the Fall and in the need for atonement. And as one would expect the word atonement in Romans 5:11 is translated reconciliation in the ERV (English Revised Version) of 1881 and in all its descendants down to this day. Westcott and his fellow translators were not orthodox enough to believe that the examples of atonement in the Old Testament foreshadowed Christ's work, or indeed that the entire Old Testament pointed toward Him.

Third, in Christology the Broad Church teaching varied from rarely held orthodoxy, to denial of the eternal Sonship, to subordinationism and Sabellianism, and on over to outright Arianism and Socinianism.

Fourth, the virgin birth was denied.

Fifth, eternal life was defined as the knowledge of God here and now on earth and did not refer to any supposed life after death. Eternal death or punishment was defined as separation from God.

Sixth, Heaven and Hell were not believed to be real places.

Seventh, the Resurrection of the Lord and His Ascension were spiritualized and made figurative. The resurrection of believers was also denied. The body was held to be only an earthly manifestation of the soul; and though the soul was immortal, there would be no resurrection of the body for either the righteous or unrighteous dead.

Eighth, the Second Coming of the Lord was taught as having happened in 70 A.D. at the fall of Jerusalem or as occurring at the death of the believer.

Ninth, verbal inspiration of the Scripture was denied, and its authority was restricted to matters of faith and practice and then only upon authentication by the reason or mind of the individual.

Tenth, the Church was taught to be the literal and only body of Christ. Christianity was said to be Christ, His Theanthropic life, continued in the Church on earth, and not any proposition or doctrine about Christ. Doctrines were consciously de-emphasized in favor of a mystical sense of union with Christ which is also to say union with the Church.

Eleventh, the incarnation was taught not as the miraculous appearance of God on earth in human flesh in the person of Jesus Christ alone, but as the union of God with all men in the unfolding of human history. The union of God with human flesh in Christ was often said to be only a type of the union of God with all men, thus universal redemption in the incarnation.

Twelfth, Darwin's theory of evolution was accepted, and the Genesis account of creation either denied or mutilated to harmonize with Darwin's ideas."[80] (HDW, my emphasis).

What heresy! And to think that Westcott and Hort (W/H) who believed the above 12 heresies, "developed" the Greek Text upon which the new modern versions are based. But we will continue to look at their lives and try to root out all possible sources of infection (leaven). The source of infection is almost as important as the infection itself. After finishing with them (W/H) we will look at the lives of others involved in this whole process before moving on to the passage of the manuscripts through the ages via two routes. We will examine where the manuscripts pick up leaven (infection) in cities and schools; and, finally, examine the Scripture and versions of the texts to see if this leaven spilled over into the 'new' Greek text and subsequently into the 'new' bible versions.

Returning to the actual quotes from Westcott and Hort we will shortly see that they believed and supported the heresies of the Broad Church. William R. Inge (1860), **a contemporary** of W/H, identified Westcott as a Broad churchman, Christian mystic, and Platonist.[81]

From the Mouth of Westcott

Westcott did not believe in miracles. He states:

> "I never read an account of a miracle but I seem instinctively to feel its improbability, and discover somewhat of evidence in the account of it."[82]

---

[80] James H. Sightler, M.D., *A Testimony Founded For Ever, The King James Bible Defended in Faith and History* (Sightler Publications, Greenville, SC, 2nd Edition, 2001) pp. 70-72.

[81] Ibid; p. 42.

[82] Gipp, op. cit., p. 217 (*Gipp's Understandable History of the Bible*).

He did not believe in the literal second coming of Jesus:

> "As far as I can remember, I said very shortly what I hold to be the 'Lord's coming' in my little book on the Historic Faith. I hold very strongly that the Fall of Jerusalem was the coming which first fulfilled the Lord's Words; and, as there have been other comings, I cannot doubt that He is 'coming' to us now,"[83]

He went all over Europe to visit the 'appearances of Mary' and believed the appearances were:

> "that of God revealing Himself, now, not in one form, but in many."[84]

His idea of heaven was, to say the least, interesting. He did not believe in a place, but like his second coming belief, spiritualized heaven. He wrote:

> "Heaven is a state and not a place. Yet the unseen is the largest part of life. Heaven lies about us now in infancy alone; and by swift, silent pauses for thought, for recollection, for aspiration, we cannot only keep fresh the influence of that diviner atmosphere, but breathe it more habitually. We may reasonably hope, by patient, resolute, faithful, united endeavor to find heaven about us here, the glory of our earthly life."[85]

He allegorized much of Scripture. He considered "Moses" and "David" poetic characters, saying:

> "No one now, I suppose, holds that the first three chapters of Genesis, for example, give a literal history — I could never understand how anyone reading them

---

[83] Ibid. p. 218.

[84] Riplinger, op. cit., p. 623 (*New Age Versions*).

[85] Gipp, op. cit. p. 218-219 (*Understandable History of the Bible*).

with open eyes could think they did – yet they disclose to us a Gospel. So it is probably elsewhere. Are we not going through a trial in regard to the use of popular language on literary subjects like that through which we went, not without sad losses in regard to the use of popular language on physical subjects? If you feel now that it was, to speak humanly, necessary that the Lord should speak of the 'sun rising,' it was no less necessary that he would use the names 'Moses" and 'David' as His contemporaries used them. There was no critical question at issue."[86]

Additional Heretical Beliefs

We could go on with multiple other quotes. One author reviewed over a thousand pages of letters and other writings by Westcott and Hort and found this kind of thinking pervasive throughout their literature. Dr. Sightler pointed out some additional weird thoughts these men had such as:

1. They would rather believe in Plato's City of Atlantis than the resurrection or the ascension.

2. They were Universalists and had abandoned the doctrine of atonement.

3. They demonstrated subordination beliefs (Jesus was subordinate to the Father) in their quotes.

4. Westcott thought eternal life was the knowledge of God here and now.[87]

---

[86] Ibid; p. 216-217.
[87] Sightler, op. cit., pp. 21-22 (*Tabernacle Essays on Bible Translation).*

The Oxford Movement

William P. Grady said in his book, *Final Authority,* that the liberal professors who took part in the Oxford movement nurtured Westcott and Hort.

> "The **Oxford Movement** or Tractarianism was an affiliation of High Church Anglicans, most of whom were members of the University of Oxford, who sought to demonstrate that the Church of England was a direct descendant of the Church established by the Apostles. It was also known as the *Tractarian Movement* after its series of publications *Tracts for the Times* (1833–1841); the Tractarians were also called **Puseyites** (usually disparagingly) after one of their leaders, Edward Bouverie Pusey, Regius Professor of Hebrew at Christ Church, Oxford. Other prominent Tractarians included John Henry Newman, a fellow of Oriel College, Oxford and vicar of the University Church of St Mary the Virgin; John Keble; Archdeacon Henry Edward Manning; Richard Hurrell Froude; Gerard Manley Hopkins; Robert Wilberforce; Isaac Williams; Charles Marriott; and Sir William Palmer."[88]

The Oxford movement was established to Romanize the Anglican Church of England; that is to turn back the wheels of time and bring the Anglican Church back under the authority of Rome and the Pope. Westcott idolized the founder of the movement, an apostate poet, John Keble (1792-1866).[89]

---

[88] http://en.wikipedia.org/wiki/Oxford_Movement.
[89] Grady, op. cit., pp. 219-220 (*Final Authority*).

The German Tubingen School

Most of the views of Westcott and Hort can be found in the thinking of the men at the German Tubingen School, Tubingen, Germany before and after these men.[90] The School was apparently a cesspool of naturalistic and rational thought, which was followed by an even worse ideology known as mysticism or Transcendentalism.[91] It infected many men who studied there including many Americans. Their unbelief was carried back to England and across the ocean to the hallowed shores of America. How sad to see such intelligent, bright men subtly overcome by the spiritual warfare that rages about all mankind second by second.

F. C. Baur (1792–1860), a Tubingen professor, who established the Tubingen School of New Testament Interpretation, taught the **mythological approach** to the Scriptures, which teaches that the concept of doctrinal truth is realized through collective myth and that the message is hidden in the myth.[92] This development followed the earlier German Rationalism and *higher criticism* (dealing with the 'ideas,' origin, and history of the original MSS whereas *lower criticism* deals with restoring the text from the MSS) that viewed miracles as impossible because nature could not be suspended. A demonstration of their apparatus for approaching what they considered a theological 'problem' would be this:

---

[90] Tubingen School of Theology, established by Ferdinand Christian Baur (1792-1860), applied the Hegelian principle to the history of early Christianity: Primitive Jewish (Petrine) Christianity, represented by the Gospel of St. Matthew, was the original force or thesis; Pauline Christianity was the antitheses of reaction against Peter—Matthew; and early Catholic Christianity according to Frederick A Norwood.

[91] Sightler, op. cit., p. 7 (*Tabernacle Essays on Bible Translation*).

[92] Ibid; pp 7-8.

"In the transcendental scheme of things the **inspiration** of Scripture is itself a myth, **an idea slowly evolving** in the mind of the early church."[93]

Spreading the Infection

Many of the ideas of the theologians in the 19th century can be traced all the way back to Origen and subsequently to Plato. Therefore, when Philip Schaff went to Germany to study under Baur's tutelage, he was infected by many of these ideas. To Philip Schaff, the Church was **the literal body** of Christ on earth and the repository of higher truth, and so, authoritative. (Does this sound like Catholicism?)

The question becomes: "What is this higher truth?" Hegel, Schelling, and Strauss further developed this idea of higher truth in the early part of the 19th century. The basic concept is that of universalism; the doctrine that the *incarnation* is God in every man and that Jesus, a myth, was a type of this incarnation. These beliefs were transmitted to **Joseph Priestly**, the discoverer of oxygen and a Unitarian, who took the principles to England. Priestly's assistant, **William Hazlett** (1784) visited **William Bently** in America who was a Harvard graduate and pastor and who subsequently led his church into Unitarianism. Hazlitt also visited a classmate of Bently's, **James Freeman**. Freeman was pastor of the first Anglican Church in America and, also, became a Unitarian.

Can you see the infection (leaven) spreading? To top all the above off, **Samuel T. Coleridge**, was a friend and associate of Priestly. It was Coleridge, a professor at Oxford, who helped Keble form and develop the Oxford movement, which infected that University with mythology, transcendentalism and Unitarianism.

---

[93] Ibid. p. 8.

The Infection Spreads to America

In America, Philip Schaff was to be chosen by Westcott and Hort to be the head of the *American Revision Committee*. There is much more that could be said about the interrelationship of all these men, and many thanks to the labors of Dr. Sightler for uncovering many of these connections.

However, let us look for a brief time at **Charles Hodge**, Princeton professor, who went to Germany (oh my!) to study. He accepted the textual approach of Griesbach, who openly denied the divinity of Christ. In addition, he accepted the short form of the Lord's prayer used in new versions.[94] [Incidentally, the short form of the Lord's Prayer is used in the Satanic Church's Bible.] Hodge was the teacher of **B. B. Warfield**, the first of the Princeton theologians to draw away from the Biblical concept of inspiration and Preservation of the Scriptures. Instead, he embraced providential restoration by textual critics and original autograph inspiration only. Warfield was the grandson of Robert J. Breckenridge who trained at Princeton under Hodge. **Breckenridge** was a leader in the Presbyterian split away from liberal New Haven Theology, a harbinger of Broad Church theology. After Breckenridge's death and his restraint of Hodge, Hodge went on to be appointed to the *American Revision Committee* and, in spite of objections to its course, acquiesced to a sifting of Scripture in America instead of 'receiving' it. **The seed of infection (leaven) begun in the Garden of Eden has continued to spread. The subtle changing of God's Words would become a full blown disease. It would accelerate like an epidemic.**

---

[94] Ibid. pp. 41-43.

Current Groups Continuing Textual Criticism

The continued influence of the corrupted texts can be see in the NT Greek studies being done by several groups around the world. For example, CSNTM ("The Center For The Study of New Testament Greek Manuscripts") and the IGNTP ("International Greek New Testament Project") are two well-known groups. The CSNTM reports:

> "To date, some 5,700 manuscripts containing about 1.3 million pages have been catalogued."

Authors have also noted that on the average about two to three new manuscripts are being found per day. There is no indication that the percentage favoring the CT or the TR/TT is changing. It is also doubtful that all of the MSS will ever be examined because of the cost, time, training of students, and other factors that enter into the equation. Furthermore, this author cannot accept that God has **hidden** His Words in MSS being continuously found in grave sites in Egypt, in monasteries in many places, and in the Vatican.

The favorite MSS of the CT men among the uncials (majuscules) have not changed. This is related to their unshakable belief that the "oldest is best." Among their other tenets, which Dean Burgon strongly criticized in *Revision Revised,* are the following, which have not really changed in spite of claims to the contrary:

I. The Basic Approach:

The basic approach that Westcott/Hort took in evaluating the manuscripts of the New Testament was to treat them **like any other book,** and they believed no new principle "whatever" was "needed or legitimate" in the approach to manuscripts. In other words, the Scripture was not "special" or received by supernatural means. The Words of Scripture would be treated like a secular book.

II. Genealogy:

According to Westcott and Hort and other textual critics, genealogy was needed to recover the texts of successive ancestors (MSS) by using analysis and comparison of the most recent texts (MSS) with prior texts. They reported that by working backwards the common ancestor could be recovered. The many manuscripts could then be reduced to one or perhaps two manuscripts. As we will see, this was never done, although they said the method had been applied. They proposed this hypothetical, never tried system in order to reduce the overwhelming majority of manuscripts that favor the Received Text (TR). Therefore, one old manuscript without any recent copies would be on the same level, or equivalent to, or as good as, or better than any recent plentiful copies of the Received Text. Now all they had to claim was that the recently recovered 'old' Codices B and Aleph were as good as or better than any recent manuscript. This is a very convenient way for a heretic to get rid of the many documents favoring the TR. Now all the families they dreamed up, the Western, the Antiochian (the Syrian), the Alexandrian, and Neutral texts, were considered equivalent because they had traced them back by genealogy to early dates. All that was left for them to do was to find a way to get rid of the "villainous" TR family and exalt the Codex B which they preferred. So, along came their next proposal.

III. Conflation:

Conflation was used to combine older text readings into one new text reading to make it a fuller and 'more pious' text. W/H went on to demonstrate eight conflated readings in the TR, but never demonstrated any in the other alleged text types. Drs. Westcoot [sic] and Hoot [sic] **invented** two meetings of early church authorities. One, they said, occurred early in Antioch, and the other about 250 to 350 AD, which conflated the Traditional or Received Text from several families of manuscripts. **There is absolutely no history of such meetings, much less a 'new' Greek text being "put together" during this time.** Dean Burgon was incensed by their attempt to fabricate the two meetings (see *Revision Revised*). Westcott and Hort tried **anything** to explain away the huge number of manuscripts with only minor scribal errors that supported the Received Text. Upon the acceptance of conflation (and therefore the acceptance of a complete [Lucian] recension in 350 A.D.) many modern textual critics such as Kirsopp Lake and Vincent Taylor have 'staked their souls'.[95]

Westcott and Hort went on to state that prior to the Church Father, Chrysostom, who died in 407, no TR (Syrian or Antiochian) reading could be found. This is a lie. This was the cornerstone of their theory, which many textual scholars still "buy into." They even carried this further by claiming the 'conflation' of the TR was done two different times. One 'conflation' of the TR was said to have occurred early in the post-Apostolic period at Antioch and the second between 250 and 350 AD. They even went so far as to suggest Lucian (d. 311) as the leader and called it the Lucian Recension. There is not one shred of

---

[95] Wilbur Pickering, Th.D., p. 37, 72 (*The Identity of the New Testament Text*).

evidence for these recensions, but the concept has gained wide acceptance among textual critics like F. C. Burkitt and H. C. Thiessen.[96] If a doctor set out to treat a patient on as 'little or no evidence' as Westcott and Hort put forth, he or she would be 'sued until the cows come home'. [A thorough discussion of all this and more can be found in Wilbur Pickering's work, *The Identity of the New Testament Text*]. In addition, Dean Burgon and others have shown in extensive detail that the TR readings existed prior to Lucian and in **many** church father quotations reaching back into the second and third centuries.[97]

IV. Textual Readings
Based Upon Internal Evidence:

The obvious simplicity of the readings in the TR caused Westcoot [sic] and Hoot [sic] to face one last problem in order to deal their attempted death blow to the text received from the **priesthood of believers.** Therefore, they invented one final significant prerequisite in their secret plan for textual scholars of the W/H school to use. The prerequisite dealt with the readings within a manuscript and it had two aspects:

1. **Brevior lectio potior** = the shorter reading is to be preferred over longer readings, and

2. **Proclivi lectioni praestat ardua** = the harder reading is to be preferred.

They allegedly constructed these two conditions based on two assumptions that could never be confirmed, which were:

---

[96] Ibid; p. 38.
[97] J. A. Moorman, *Early Church Fathers and the Authorized Version: A Demonstration!*, Companion Volume to *Early Manuscripts and the Authorized Version;* Moorman's work supports the early quotes of the RT Text.

1. The tendency of scribes to add material to the text, and

2. The tendency of scribes to simplify the text when confronted with a difficult reading.

The real reason the prerequisites were "developed" and, incidentally, they were only **a theory which could not be established by testing or research,** was to get rid of the TR.

So, what do you imagine they said about the readings in the TR? That's right; they were too simple and they were too long. They were a "full text," meaning the text had been added to, and they exhibited "harmonistic assimilation," meaning they had been simplified. Now the readings in the TR could be thrown out in favor of the readings in Westcott and Hort's 'new' Greek text.

The critical apparatus which Westcott and Hort developed was primarily established on a concept called "Genealogy." Based on their research, they claimed the transmission of the New Testament text occurred through families. The deceit is this: THEY NEVER APPLIED THEIR 'THEORY' TO THE MANUSCRIPTS *AS THEY HAD CLAIMED TO HAVE DONE.* Wilbur Pickering in his thesis for Dallas Theological Seminary reports the following:

> "M.M. Parvis answers: "Westcott and Hort never applied the genealogical method to the NT MSS..." Colwell agrees. [Colwell said:]
> "That Westcott and Hort did *not* apply this method to the manuscripts of the New Testament is obvious. Where are the charts which start with the majority of late manuscripts and climb back through diminishing generations of ancestors to the Neutral and Western texts? The answer is that they are nowhere. Look again at the first diagram, and you will see that ....[they] are not actual manuscripts of the New Testament, but hypothetical manuscripts. The demonstrations or illustrations of the genealogical method as applied to New Testament manuscripts by

the followers of Hort,…use hypothetical manuscripts, not actual codices. …All the manuscripts referred to are *imaginary* manuscripts, and the later of these charts was printed sixty years after Hort."

How then could Hort speak of only "occasional ambiguities in the evidence for the genealogical relation," or say the following?

"So far as genealogical relations are discovered with perfect certainty, the textual results which follow from them are perfectly certain, too, being directly involved in historical facts; and any apparent presumptions against them suggested by other methods are mere guesses against knowledge." [then Pickering says:] when he had *not* demonstrated the existence of any such relations, much less with "perfect certainty?"[98] [HDW, Because he lied][HDW, my emphasis]

Another prevarication is that Westcott and Hort declared the readings of the traditional text were absent from the writings of the Anti-Nicene Fathers. Wilbur Pickering said, "Dr. Hort draws largely from his imagination and wishes" concerning absent readings.[99] Even recent textual critics deny the evidence of patristic quotes and slant their reporting, although *many* researchers have shown church fathers quotes support the TR.[100] Dean Burgon, Westcott and Hort's contemporary, destroyed all their arguments, but his information was disregarded by the well-known modern technique of "spin."

Another disconcerting aspect of this approach by W/H is the myth asserted by them and their followers "that the true New

---

[98] Wilbur Pickering,Th.D., *The Identity of the New Testament Text* (Thomas Nelson Publishers, Nashville, TN, Revised Edition available through The Bible for Today, #556, Collingswood, NJ).
[99] Pickering, op. cit., p. 66.
[100] Ibid; pp. 69-70.

Testament text was lost for more than 1500 years and then restored by Westcott and Hort."[101]

A 30 Year Secret

For over 30 years, Westcott and Hort had been preparing, *in secret,* a Greek text to replace the Greek Received Text. To accomplish this feat, they also developed a new critical apparatus to be used by textual critics. The Convocation of the Southern Province of Great Britain specifically instructed them to change *only* "the plain and clear errors" in the Greek Text. "To construct a 'new' Greek Text *formed no part of the Instructions* which the Revisionists received at the hands of the Convocation of the Southern Province."[102] Westcott and Hort directly disobeyed and rebelled against authority and fraudulently paraded before the committee, piece-by-piece, their scheme that was hatched over thirty years to "cast on the world" a 'new' Greek text because of their revulsion for the Received Text. Their coercion and intimidation of those on the committee was made possible because of their positions at institutions of higher learning, which in and of itself is revolting.

The effects of this spirit of rebellion, which the Scriptures says is as witchcraft, [1Sam 15:23] has led to long term effects which will be discussed later. Westcott and Hort had agreed to the terms of the Convocation, but intentionally hid their plans in order to get the meetings started.

---

[101] Hills, op. cit. p. 194 (*The King James Version Defended*).
[102] David Otis Fuller, *True or False* (Grand Rapids International Publications, 1990 Institute for Biblical Textual Studies, ISBN 0-944355-12-9, 1995) p.129.

The 'New" Version From W/H 'New' Greek Text

The committee Drs. Hoot [sic] and Westcoot [sic] controlled, simultaneously produced a new English translation from their 'new' Greek text, called, *The Revised Version*. It is also known as the ERV, the *English Revised Version*. It was produced against the authority and rules established that were to govern the committee. I have in my possession a copy of the Revised Version of 1885, which is a family Bible, passed down through the generations of our family. The wording in the preface to this old Bible, which is Westcott and Hort's version, leads one to believe it is just an updating of the King James Bible (KJB) of 1611. It is not "just" an updating of the KJB resulting from the discovery of 'older' manuscripts, but is a completely 'new' version. I personally consider this another subtle deception.

Inexplicable Favoritism

How could these men intentionally set aside overwhelming evidence that is in support of the RT/TT in favor of a new constructed Greek Text and a new translation from that text? It had to be the influence of evil spiritual forces. For example, note the evidence of lectionaries alone. A lectionary in the early church was a grouping of Scriptures to be read in the church service. There is not one of them that favors the CT. One hundred percent of them favor the RT/TT.

Furthermore, the following information adds to the mystery of their decisions. Conflation is the intentional embellishing or combining of the text of Scripture to make it sound more 'pious' and as a result 'fuller.' An example would be the addition of Lord and Christ to the name Jesus to make it read—the Lord Jesus Christ. Eight examples of conflation were allegedly found in the RT/TT and reported by Westcott and Hort, and no more, although they intimated many more were present. Textual Critics to this day have not found any more and Dean Burgon eliminated most of the eight W/H had supposedly found.[103] Westcott and Hort would have you believe that at least 20% of the Received Text has been conflated.

Adding to all of this subterfuge, is a profound admission by the committee chairman of the Anglican Convocation of the Southern Province, Bishop Charles Ellicott. He did not believe there was enough 'knowledge' among the committee members to change the Greek Text. In 1861, Bishop Ellicott said:

> "It is my honest conviction that for any authoritative REVISION, we are not yet mature; *either in Biblical learning or Hellenistic scholarship.* There is good scholarship in this country,...*but it has certainly not yet been sufficiently directed to the study of the New Testament...*to render any national attempt at REVISION either hopeful or lastingly profitable."[104]

A Caution

The significant failure of every generation is the neglect of the clear proclamation of God that we are to be wary of any "facts" or "truths" that are not supported by Scripture.

> *"The simple believeth every word: but the prudent man looketh well to his going." Proverbs 14:15, cf. 1 Jn. 4:1, Jos. 9:14, Gen. 3:5-6).*

Many individuals do not retreat from:

---

[103] Pickering, op. cit., p. 61 (*The Identity of the New Testament Text*).
[104] William P. Grady, Ph.D.,Th.M., D.D., p. 252 (*Final Authority*).

"the presence of a foolish man when [they] perceivest not in him the lips of knowledge" (Pro. 14:7).

In this verse, "knowledge" is understanding, wisdom, and prudence **from God's Words** that comes from the lips of a person; that is, his "speak" contains God's Words properly applied.

CHAPTER 3

THE MANUSCRIPTS

What I believe about the Bible cannot be better stated than the way Dean John William Burgon stated it in 1861:

> "But this day's Sermon,...has had for its object to remind you, that THE BIBLE is none other than *the voice of Him that sitteth upon the Throne!* Every Book of it,—every Chapter of it,—every Verse of it,—every word of it,—every syllable of it,—(*where* are we to *stop?)*—every letter of it—is the direct utterance of the *Most* High! Pasa graphé theopneustos. "Well spake the Holy Ghost, by the mouth of" the many blessed Men who wrote it.—The Bible is none other than *the Word of God:* not some part of it, more, some part of it, less; but all alike, the utterance of Him who sitteth upon the Throne;--absolute,--faultless,--unerring,--supreme![105]

This one statement alone counters the false declarations frequently reported on the internet as to Dean Burgon's belief about the text behind the Bible and the King James Bible translation that was in common use. There are many who come against the Dean Burgon Society (DBS) and state that Dean Burgon would not belong to the DBS. How wrong they are! The DBS believes what Dean Burgon believes about the Bible. His statement reflects what we are to believe about the Bible from the Bible itself (Mat. 4:4, 24:35, 2 Tim. 3:15-17, etc.).

---

[105] Dean John William Burgon, *Inspiration and Interpretation* (Dean Burgon Society Press, Collingwood, NJ, 1999, originally published 1861 by J. H. and Jas. Parker) p. 89.

Anyone not holding to these concepts and beliefs about the Bible are subject to supporting the CT and the 'scholars' who vigorously put forth modern textual criticism. They claim textual criticism is the answer for *reconstructing* all the MSS in order to come very close to the original MSS that emanated directly from the pens of the apostles and prophets. Without the originals, this is impossible; it is reconstruction without the pattern, something that is not possible. For example, reconstructing an original "Ford" automobile without any original by examining several modified, "molded," or modern models is impossible. Rather, by *recognizing* the relatively few unintentional errors, such as spelling and similar errors in the majority of virtually identical MSS, the church has demonstrated the preservation of the inerrant *Received Texts*. This is similar to fixing a few dents in a copy of the original Ford automobile. However, a problem may arise as to which "dent" was intentional or unintentional. By far, the differences in RT/TT MSS are simply spelling errors, but occasionally further research is needed. Certainly, the RT/TT should NEVER be changed unless Dean Burgon's seven notes of Truth are followed (see Burgon's *The Traditional Text of the Holy Scriptures*).

An Example of Corruption

This begs for an example from Scripture, which raises the question of whether the corruption in the CT was intentional or unintentional. The reason it is presented, is to admit RT/TT men cannot always be certain whether a corruption in a text is intentional or unintentional. However, if it is in a MSS which demonstrates multiple corruptions that favor Gnostic beliefs, then it has to be accepted as being compatible with the general tendencies of the Gnostics and CT men who, knowingly or unknowingly, spread the disease of textual criticism.

Gloria in excelsis deo is a popular hymn based upon a corrupted text in the Latin MSS at Lk. 2:14. Pope Symmachus (498-514) introduced this hymn into the opening rites for the Mass on Sundays and major feast days. It is, therefore, most commonly known as one of the ordinary chants of the Mass.

> Glory to God in the highest, and on earth peace to people of good will."

> *"Glory to God in the highest, and on earth peace, good will toward men." Luke 2:14*

The false reading came about because of a scribal mistake, whether intentional or not, we don't know. If I had to guess, I would suppose that it was a series of mistakes. First an "en" in Greek was left out, and then a grammarian, perhaps Jerome, knew the text did not read correctly and subsequently changed a noun to an adjective.

Uncials and Cursives

The modernistic textual critic claims the discipline of modern textual criticism arose because of the thousands of differences in the words of Greek MSS. They claim the MSS are extant in several different forms and alleged families, which is not true. There is only one family and a few corrupted MSS. However, there are certain considerations.

The way the letters are formed is the first consideration. Some MSS exist as uncials, which are capital letters. Phil. 1:1-2, in Greek, would read something like this:

ΠΑΥΛΟΣΚΑΙΤΙΜΟΘΕΟΣΔΟΥΛΟΙΙΗΣΟΥΧΡΙΣΤΟΥΠΑ
ΣΙΤΟΙΣΑΓΙΟ ΙΣΕΝΧΡΙΣΤΩΙΗΣΟΥΤΟΙΣΟΥΣΙΝΕΝΦΙΛΙΠ
ΠΟΙΣΣΥΝΕΠΙΣΚΟΠΟ ΙΣΚΑΙΔΙΑΚΟΝΟΙΣΧΑΡΙΣΥΜΙΝ
ΚΑΙΕΙΡΗΝΗΑΠΟΘΕΟΥΠΑΤΡΟΣΗ ΜΩΝΚΑΙΚΥΡΙΟΥΙ
ΗΣΟΥΧΡΙΣΤΟΥ

When translated into English, the reading is still difficult.

PAULANDTIMOTHEUSTHESERVANTSOFJESUSCH
RISTTOALLTHESAINTSINCHRISTJESUSWHICHAR
EATPHILIPPIWITHTHEBISHOPSANDDEACONSGR
ACEBEUNTOYOUANDPEACEFROMGODOURFATH
ERANDFROMTHELORDJESUSCHRIST"[106]

Here it is in Spanish.

PABLOYTIMOTEOSIERVOSDEJESUSCRUSTOATO
DOSLOSSANTOSENCRISTOJESUSQUEESTANENF
ILIPOSCONLOSOBISPOSYDIACONOSGRACIASEA
AVOSOTROSYPAZDEDIOSNUESTROPADREYDEL
SENORJESUCRISTO.

The old uncial MSS such as B and Aleph still exist because they were not used. They were not used because men knew they were corrupt. If they had been used regularly, they would have deteriorated. My Bible, which is constructed with much better materials than those used in ancient times, is in serious need of rebinding after a few years of use. When Tischendorf found the Sinaiticus MSS in the Monastery of St. Catherine, located in the middle of the desert, it was in a trash

---

[106] Holland, op. cit., (*Crowned With Glory The Bible From The Ancient Texts to the Authorized Version*, Chapter 2, Monarch of Books).

can, the contents of which the monks were burning in order to stay warm. It was of no use because it was so corrupt that the monks believed it could be better used as fuel for a fire. These facts should cause anyone to pause who uses a Bible based upon these old uncials such as B and Aleph.

Other MSS are cursives, which are more like the longhand letter of today. It is often reported that the cursive MSS followed the uncial MSS technique. But that is not true. They overlapped. However, the cursive MSS won out as the technique for copying and there are subsequently far more cursives than uncials.

A second consideration is the way they were stored. Many MSS were kept by the owner as scrolls, which were MSS rolled up and tied. The other way they were kept by their owners was as codices, which were sheets bound together at an edge much like a book is bound today.

The primary materials that MSS were written upon were first, papyrus, a paper-like material made from reeds growing near river banks and second, parchments made from animal hides. The codices were called lectionaries if they were organized as portions of Scriptures to be read in a church. Occasionally, codices were translations of the New Testament books into regional languages such as Aramaic, Coptic (Egyptian), Latin, Armenian, Gothic, etc. The Septuagint or LXX is a Greek translation of the Old Testament and contains the apocrypha.

A papyrus codex was fragile and deteriorated quickly with use, which required frequent recopying. An animal hide codex was very expensive. They tended to last longer, but deterioration still occurred relatively rapidly also because the inks faded, the material dried out and cracked, or they were used as a rescriptus; that is, the writing on them was washed off and the hide used again. These facts become very important when considering the arguments of the modernistic textual critic and their reconstruction of the Greek New Testament.[107] We have thousands of MSS of the Bible; far more than for any secular book. The total number of MSS that corroborate the Bible was recently reported as 24,000.[108] Furthermore, substantiation of the readings for the RT/TT is affirmed by many more church elder quotes than for the CT.

> "But possibly the greatest attestation for the authority of our New Testament are the masses of quotations taken from its pages by the early church fathers. Dean Burgon in his research found in all **86,489** quotes from the early church fathers (McDowell 1990:47-48; 1991:52). In fact, there are **32,000** quotations from the New Testament found in writings from before the council of Nicea in 325 A.D. (Mcdowell Evidence, 1972:52). J. Harold Greenlee points out that the quotations of the scripture in the

---

[107] "A picture depicting the 10th century Aleppo Codex is displayed during a news conference at Jerusalem's Yad Ben-Zvi institute December 2, 2007. The institute said last month that a 1,000-year-old parchment, the size of a credit card, forms part of the Aleppo Codex, viewed by scholars as one of the most authoritative manuscripts of the Hebrew bible. The parchment was kept as a lucky charm by Sam Sabbagh, a Syrian Jew who in 1947 plucked it from the floor of an Aleppo synagogue that was torched after a United Nations decision to partition Palestine, paving the way for the creation of Israel.
http://images.google.com/imgres?imgurl=http://cache.daylife.com/imageserve/07Dk8275kc1VY/610x.jpg&imgrefurl=http://www.daylife.com/photo/07Dk8275kc1VY&h=393&w=610&sz=64&hl=en&start=119&um=1&usg=__twNa0GZBcO2lDdb14IgdGWHzVJg=&tbnid=EvUZWBJJSb5RSM:&tbnh=88&tbnw=136&prev=/images%3Fq%3Da%2BBible%2Bcodex%26start%3D108%26ndsp%3D18%26um%3D1%26hl%3Den%26rls%3DGGLD,GGLD:2004-04,GGLD:en%26sa%3DN, accessed 10/2008.
[108] http://debate.org.uk/topics/history/bib-qur/bibmanu.htm

works of the early church writers are so extensive that the New Testament could virtually be reconstructed from them without the use of New Testament manuscripts."[109]

The Necessity for a Pattern

We do not agree with the last statement by J. Harold Greenlee concerning reconstruction of the text because without a "pattern" as a guide, the Scripture can not and could not be reconstructed, no matter how sincere a man's attempt might be. This is one of the most important issues, difficulties, and problems for the textual critic. The question for them is, "How can they arrive at the "original" New Testament Greek words, if they do not have the original?"

Obviously, subjectivism becomes a major component of modern textual criticism since we do not have the original MSS. This is called "conjectural emendation" by modernistic textual critics; in other words, guessing, speculation, or gambling about which Words of a Living God are the inspired Words. That is exactly what we discover when the tenets of modern textual criticism are evaluated. Dean John William Burgon (1823-1888) destroyed the postulates of *subjective* modern textual critics who were primarily German, French, English, Italian, and Swedish 'scholars' (q.v., Chapter 2). Throughout Scripture, man is cautioned not to speculate, guess at, or propose his own words as if they were the Words of God (Deut. 4:3, Prov. 30:5-6, Rev. 22:18-19, Isa. 59:13-14, Jer. 7:4, 8).

---

[109] http://debate.org.uk/topics/history/bib-qur/bibmanu.htm

Two Ways to Evaluate Scriptural Texts

There are basically two approaches to evaluation of the texts of Scripture—believing or unbelieving. The tenets that developed or evolved from the two routes are very important for pastors, teachers, and the layman to understand because the texts that result from the two methods differ drastically and severely. Furthermore, the men who support or are invovled in the two streams are significantly and considerably different in their theology, philosophy of life, and bibliology (see Chapter 2).

Some scholars claim that critical tenets were not used in the route that resulted in the RT/TT. They are partly right. The men responsible for the RT/TT did NOT use "criticism" or "censoring" of the text from a "conjectural emendation" approach or point of view (see below); rather, they used facts to assemble, weigh, and balance different kinds of evidence. Dr. Jeffrey Khoo, Dean of the Far Eastern Bible College, said:

> "Knowing where the perfect Bible is is a matter of textual recognition and NOT textual criticism."[110]

It bears repeating that most problems, if they can be called problems, in the MSS of the RT/TT route are spelling differences.

What one believes concerning the origin of the Critical Text depends on one's point of view. That is, if you are a Traditional Text

---

[110] Rev. Dennis Kwok *et al.*, *VPP of the Bible, A Course on the Doctrine of Verbal Plenary Preservation* (The Old Paths Publications, Cleveland, GA, 2008) 21.

(TT) man, you believe the CT began *"in the beginning"* (q.v.) and the influence of the instigator (Satan) continues to manipulate men.

The following quote from *The International Standard Bible Encyclopedia* is typical of men who favor the CT.

> But the Textus Receptus of the New Testament (Stephanus' 3rd edition in 1550) was the basis of the King James Version of 1611. This edition of the Greek New Testament made use of **a very few manuscripts, and all of them late**, except Codex Bezae, which was considered too eccentric to follow. Practically, then, the King James Version represents the Syriac type of text which may have been edited in Antioch in the 4th century. Various minor errors may have crept in since that date, but substantially the Syriac recension is the text of the King James Version today. Where this text stands alone, it is held by nearly all modern scholars to be in error, though Dean Burgon fought hard for the originality of the Syriac text (The Revision Revised, 1882). The text of Westcott and Hort, The New Testament in Greek is practically that of Codex Vaticanus, which is held to be the Neutral type of text. Nestle, von Soden, Weiss do not differ greatly from the text of Westcott and Hort, The New Testament in Greek, though von Soden and Weiss attack the problem on independent lines. The text of the Revised Version (British and American) is in a sense a compromise between that of the King James Version and the Critical Text, though coming pretty close to the Critical Text. Compare Whitney, The Reviser's Greek Text, 1892. For a present-day appreciation of this battle of the texts see J. Rendel Harris, Side Lights on the New Testament, 1908. For a detailed comparison between the King James Version and the Revised Version (British and American) Acts see Rackham, The Acts of the Apostles, xxii."[111]

---

[111] James Orr, M.A., D.D., General Editor John L. Nuelsen, D.D., LL.D., Edgar Y. Mullins, D.D., LL.D., Assistant Editors Morris O. Evans, D.D., PhD., Managing Editor Melvin Grove Kyle, D.D., JJ.D. Revising Editor, *International Standard Bible Encyclopedia* (SwordSearcher, Version 5.4.1.2,

Note the disparaging of the RT/TT as being constructed from a few late MSS. This is not true and it is an outright lie. The first to print the RT/TT was Erasmus, an unparalleled scholar who traveled to: 1. the Vatican, 2. many countries, and 3. many libraries, to examine the MSS. He consulted with many other scholars and protectors of 'received-type' MSS. He rejected the CT-type readings from B and Aleph as did the editors of the RT/TT such as Stephanus, the Elzivers, Beza, and the KJB translators who followed him. Erasmus selected a few MSS that best represented the RT/TT; that is, had fewer differences among them.

The Families

The world of textual criticism has divided the ancient New Testament manuscripts into classes or families of texts. There is disagreement among them as to the proper classification, as one would expect, but here are the most popular 'families.' If someone wants to be a "classifier," an extensive knowledge of the original languages and dialects is needed. However, do not be led to believe that if you do not have linguistic talents, you cannot understand the concepts. James White, a CT man, lists the types.

> "They are:
> **The Alexandrian text-type**, found in most papyri, and in the great uncial codices Aleph and B.
> **The Western text-type**, found both in Greek manuscripts and in translations into other languages, especially Latin.
> **The Byzantine text-type**, found in the vast majority of later uncial and minuscule manuscripts.

Broken Arrow, OK, originally published, 1939, 2008) Acts of the Apostles, The Text.

The Caesarean text-type, disputed by some, found in P45 and "family 1" (abbreviated f^1)"[112] (HDW, my emphasis).

The question naturally arises as to how these text-types developed. There are two suppositions.

1. During the first two centuries immediately after the writing of the New Testament books, there was a tremendous "attack" on the written Words. Satan was not successful discrediting the Living Word so he turned his attention to the inspired Words. This was accomplished by using men who did not have respect toward the Words of God the way the Old Testament scribes of Israel did. They had no problem with changing the wording so that it better fit their philosophy. Those making the changes were primarily Gnostics and as we shall see, the Alexandrian, Origen, was an Arian and a Gnostic.

2. Copyist errors occurred. These type errors have always been a problem when copying anything. However, the tremendous demand for copies of the epistles and gospels while the church was under horrendous persecution caused more than the usual scribal errors. 'Scholars' claim the MSS can be placed into families based on persistent errors in copies in certain regions such as Western, Syrian, Egyptian, etc.

Errors and Alterations

To summarize: There were intentional and unintentional errors. Many have denied the intentional errors because there were no proofs. Westcott and Hort were among those who claimed "no intentional errors." If there were, W/H knew it would destroy their

---

[112] James White, *The King James Only Controversy* (Bethany House Publishers, Minneapolis, Minn.; ISBN 1-55661-575-2) p. 43.

theory of genealogy. MSS cannot be traced in "families" if intentional corruptions occurred. It is like trying to find a location if someone lies to you about where it is. However, intentional errors were made. Among intentional errors, there were those that were made in 'good faith' to make the text more understandable or conformable to another "older" reading and those that were made to satisfy a requirement of someone's belief system.

Bruce Metzger describes an example of a "good faith" error. He relates that in the margin of codex Vaticanus at Hebrews 1:3 there is a rather:

> "indignant note by a recent scribe who restored the original reading of the codex...for which a corrector had substituted the usual reading...[which said] "Fool and knave, can't you leave the old reading alone and not alter it!"[113]

Alterations in the text, made because of doctrinal considerations, are difficult to judge, but they were made. Irenaeus, Tertullian, Eusebius, and many other church Fathers complained about the corrupting of Scripture by the heretics:

> "In the mid-second century Marcion expunged his copies of the Gospel according to Luke of all references to the Jewish background of Jesus. Tatian's *Harmony of the Gospels* contains several textual alterations which lent support to ascetic or encratite [sic] views."[114]

According to Metzger, eliminating what was considered unacceptable doctrinally, or inserting what was necessary to "prove" a

---

[113] Bruce Metzger, *The Text of the New Testament* pp. 195- 196.
[114] Ibid; p. 201.

tenet, was not unusual. He then goes on to give several examples, not only in manuscripts related to Scripture, but in lay literature such as *The Pilgrim's Progress*.[115]

Previously, we discussed the kinds of unintentional errors such as haplography, dittography, fission, etc. So it is easy to see how variants would occur. The question arises as to the classification of those variants into *different* families. We will give a brief discussion of those "families" and then look at the origin of the concept.

Classification Into Families

The Western text family is alleged to have arisen "in the better educated Christian circles."[116] It is reasoned that these persons were better able to write, and subsequently, made comments in the margins of their text. When these annotated manuscripts were copied, the comments were incorporated into the text.

The Alexandrian family characteristics are said to have developed for different reasons:

> "Among the Christian scribes of Alexandria developments took another turn. According to Streeter (1924), these learned Christians followed the tradition of Alexandrian classical scholarship, which was always to prefer the shortest reading in places in which the manuscripts differed. The Alexandrians were always ready to suspect and reject New Testament readings which seemed to them to present difficulties. John Burgon (1896), one of England's greatest believing Bible scholars, proved this long ago by pointing out a relevant passage in Origen's Commentary on Matthew.

---

[115] Ibid; pp. 195-207.
[116] Moorman, op. cit. p. 53 (*Forever Settled*).

"In this Commentary, Origen, the leading Christian critic of antiquity, gives us an insight into the arbitrary and highly subjective manner in which New Testament textual criticism was carried on at Alexandria about 230 A.D. In his comment on Matt. 19: 17-21 (Jesus' reply to the rich young man) Origen reasons that Jesus could not have concluded his list of God's commandment with the comprehensive requirement, Thou shalt love thy neighbour as thyself. For the reply of the young man was, All these things have I kept from my youth up, and Jesus evidently accepted this statement as true. But if the young man had loved his neighbor as himself, he would have been perfect, for Paul says that the whole law is summed up in this saying, Thou shalt love thy neighbour as thyself. But Jesus answered, If thou wilt be perfect etc., implying that the young man was not yet perfect. Therefore, Origen argued, the commandment, Thou shalt love thy neighbour as thyself, could not have been spoken by Jesus on this occasion and was not part of the original text of Matthew. The clause had been added, Origen concluded, by some tasteless scribe."[117]

Bruce Metzger points out that Westcott and Hort developed the naturalist neutral approach to classifying the texts of the New Testament into families. Metzger, like most modern textual critics, has blindly accepted the "theories" of Westcott and Hort because they think like calculators, or computers, or cold fish. He is also a heretic. "In the introductions to the books of the *Reader's Digest Bible*, Metzger questions the authorship, traditional date, and supernatural inspiration of books penned by Moses, Daniel, and Peter, and in many other ways reveals his liberal, unbelieving heart...He piously claims on one hand that the Bible is the inspired Words of God; but out of the other side of the mouth he claims the Bible is filled with myth and error. He denies the Bible's history, its miracles, and its authorship, while, in true liberal style, declaring that this denial does not do injustice to the Words of God, because, he says, the

---

[117] Ibid; p. 53.

Bible is not "written for history but for religion" and is not to be read "with a dull prosaic and literalistic mind"![118]

The Truth About Families

The truth is there is really only one family. I took you through the preceding concepts to show how following the logic of the naturalist's textual criticism can easily mislead anyone. By now you were probably thinking all the above sounds good, correct, and true. THE TRUTH IS THERE IS BUT ONE FAMILY OF TEXTS, THE RECEIVED TEXT. All the other texts are very confusing and differ from one another to a great extent. This fact can be illustrated by Herman Hoskier's research, which showed that there were over 3000 differences between Codex Vaticanus and Codex Alexandrinus **in the gospels alone.** To claim that they can be placed into families is fabricated and arbitrary. In other words, the classification of manuscripts by textual critics is an area which produces great dissention even among the textual critics and turns out to be based on purely ***personal opinion.*** The concept also provides a critic with many hours of idle conjecture. That there are a few similarities between a few corrupted texts because of recopying cannot be refuted, but a 'family' it does not make:

> "Though there is [some] truth in the above commonly presented position and we have quoted Dr. Hills at length, yet the basic idea of textual types or families has its source in the naturalistic viewpoint and we do not believe that it represents the facts concerning the distribution of MSS [manuscript**s**] in the early

---

[118] David Cloud, "Unholy Hands on God's Holy Book, A Report on the United Bible Society" (Way of Life Literature, email 1985; Part I of II;, May 2000).

centuries. With some 85% or more of the 5000 extant MSS falling into the category of the Received Text, **there is in fact only one textual family – the Received.** All that remains is so contradictory, so confused, so mixed, that not by the furthest stretch of imagination can they be considered several families of MSS."[119] [HDW, my emphasis]

There is a strong suspicion on my part that Westcott and Hort devised the "family" approach in order to confuse the ordinary person by disguising the fact that there are so few MSS to support their position. Even the word "family" connotes the sense of 'numbers', suggesting to a person there are a lot of MSS in this or that category.

However, there are few (approximately 1%). What follows are the most popular MSS of the modern textual critic. Most of this information comes from the work of Dr. J. A. Moorman; particularly, his book, *Forever Settled.*

Papyrus Manuscripts

The most significant papyrus MSS are the P45 (3rd Century), P46 (known as the Chester Beaty Papyri, c. 200), P66 (c. 200), and P75 (known as the "Bodmer Papyrus II", 3rd Century). Jack Moorman says these are the "favorite sons" of the modern textual critic. Remember, the papyrus fragments come primarily from Egypt where the dry climate favors their preservation. The result of analysis of these documents shows some interesting features, which is astounding in light of their source. The papyri fragments show readings that favor the:

---

[119] Moorman, op. cit., p. 205 (*Forever Settled*).

Sinaiticus	60 times
Vaticanus	124 times
Received Text	**139 times**[120]

Uncial Manuscripts

There are about 267 extant uncial manuscripts which contain parts of the New Testament, but only 5 which are alleged to be "the oldest and best." Below is the list with where they are currently located.

Manuscript (Codex)	Century Copied	Location	Contents
1. Aleph (Sinaiticus)	IV	London	Gospels, Acts, Epistles, Revelation
2. Alexandrinus	V	London	Gospels, Acts, Epistles, Revelation; minus portions of Matthew, John, & II Corinthians
3. B (Vaticanus)	IV	Rome	Gospels, Acts, Epistles, (minus portions of 1 Timothy, Philemon, Hebrews
4. C	V	Paris	Portions of all the

---

[120] Ibid. p. 78.

(Ephaermi Rescriptus)			NT books
5. D (Beza) (Cantabrigiensiss)	V	Cambridge	Portions of Gospels, Acts, James, & Jude

These five manuscripts are the ones favored by modern textual critics. Aleph and B also contain apocryphal books, which indicates they most likely came from Origen's *Hexapla* and the fifth column in it, which was the Septuagint (LXX).[121]

There are only these five uncial MSS and a few others, which primarily support the modern versions of the 'bible,' but even then, not completely. Many passages in the five MSS are 'received text-type.' The favorite of most modern textual critics is B (Vaticanus) located in the Vatican. In 1864, Dr. Scrivener published *"A Full Collation of the Codex Sinaiticus"* in which he states in the introduction that:

> "the Codex is covered with such alterations" (i.e., alterations of an obviously correctional character) "brought in **by at least ten different revisers**, some of them systematically spread over every page, others occasional, or limited to separate portions of the Ms., many of these being contemporaneous with the first writer, but for the greater part belonging to the sixth or seventh century."

Commenting on the five codices, Dean Burgon says:

> "The impurity of the text exhibited by these codices is not a question of opinion but of fact .... In

---

[121] H. D. Williams, M. D., Ph.D., "The Septuagint" (you can find this article on the William Carey Bible Society's website: http://wcbible.org/index.html.

the Gospels alone Codex B (Vatican) leaves out words or whole clauses no less than 1,491 times. It bears traces of careless transcription on every page. Codex Sinaiticus 'abounds with errors of the eye and pen to an extent not indeed unparalleled, but happily rather unusual in documents of first-rate importance.' On many occasions 10, 20, 30, 40 words are dropped through very carelessness. Letters and words, even whole sentences, are frequently written twice over, or begun and immediately cancelled; while that gross blunder, whereby a clause is omitted because it happens to end in the same word as the clause preceding, occurs no less than 115 times in the New Testament."

"In enumerating and describing the five ancient Codices now in existence, Dean Burgon remarks that four of these, and especially the Vatican and Sinaitic Mss. "have, within the last twenty years, established a tyrannical ascendancy over the imagination of the critics which can only be fitly spoken of as blind superstition.

"Dean Burgon, whom we shall have occasion to quote largely because of his mastery of the entire subject, after having spent **five and a half years** "laboriously collating the five old uncials throughout the Gospels," declared at the completion of his prodigious task that

"So manifest are the disfigurements jointly and exclusively exhibited by the two codices (Vatican and Sinaitic) that, instead of accepting them as two independent witnesses to the inspired original, we are constrained to regard them as little more than a single reproduction of one and the same scandalously corrupt and comparatively late Copy."

"As a sufficient illustration of the many differences between these two Codices and the great body of other MSS, we note that, in the Gospels alone, Codex Vaticanus differs from the Received Text in the following particulars: It omits at least 2,877 words; it adds 536 words; it substitutes 935 words; it transposes 2,098 words; and it modifies 1,132; making a total of 7,578 verbal divergences. But the Sinaitic Ms. is even worse, for its total divergences in the particulars stated above amount to nearly nine thousand.

These are strong statements, but the facts on which they are based seem fully to warrant them. Therefore it matters not what specific excellencies might be attributed to the Revised Version of the New Testament, the fact that the underlying Greek Text was fashioned in conformity to the Mss. referred to in the above quoted paragraph is reason enough why it should be shunned by Bible users."[122]

This concludes a brief look at the papyrus and uncial manuscripts.

Any serious student of the Scriptures needs to appropriate the fact that all the lectionaries favor the TR/TT. Furthermore, approximately two thirds (66%) of the quotes of Scripture by Anti-Nicene church fathers (before 325 AD) favor the RT/TT.

Conclusion

There are five significant pivotal points in the origin of the CT.

1. The initiator of the devious disrespect for God's Words began with that old serpent the Devil (Gen. 3, and Mat. 4).

2. The two centuries immediately after the completion of the NT were the most significant period for the attack on the Canon of Scripture. The center for the attacks was Alexandria, Egypt where dozens of cults thrived. In addition, Origen, the greatest corrupter of Scripture, began his devious changing of the Words of God to fit his philosophy and beliefs. He was a prolific writer who was supported by a wealthy Alexandrian, Ambrosius. He even traveled to parts of the

---

[122] Dean John William Burgon, *Revision Revised* (Anyone interested in the corrupted critical text, its origin and transmission, should read this book, and so the page numbers are not given.) The book may be order from Amazon.com published by The Old Paths Publications.

known world with an entourage of scribes who changed copies of the MSS. Dr. Floyd Nolan Jones, an excellent scholar and chronologist, reports this information from Eusebius' *Ecclesiastical History,* Bk. VI, Ch. 23; Elgin S. Moyer's *Who Was Who in Church History,* p. 315; and John Reumann's, *The Romance of Bible Scripts and Scholars,* pp. 98-103; that:

> "Origen traveled extensively and everywhere he found a Greek New Testament, it was altered to fit his doctrine. He, of course, felt that he was merely "correcting" the manuscripts. However, men of God do not change original manuscript readings....Origen had a wealthy patron (Ambrosius) who supplied over seven stenographers, as many copyists, and girls skilled in calligraphy to accompany and assist him as he systematically altered Scripture."[123]

3. The third significant pivotal point was Jerome's production of the Latin Vulgate. Many authors, including Bruce Metzger, have reported that Jerome used the local Alexandrian text-type MSS. David Cloud noted that the Latin Vulgate is a half-way house between B and Aleph and the TR. The Latin Vulgate has had a significant influence in history, partly because the Roman Catholic Church was such a threat to anyone who did not agree with them (e.g. consider Wycliffe, Luther, Tyndale, Huss, and thousands of others).

4. The fourth pivotal point is the publication of Charles Darwin's *The Origin of Species* in 1857.

5. The fifth pivotal point was the construction of the Westcott/Hort 'new' Greek text and the translation from it called the *English Revised Version* in the 1880's.

---

[123] Floyd Nolan Jones, *Which Version Is The Bible?* (KingsWord Press, Goodyear, AZ, 19th Edition, First Edition 1989) p. 93.

The culmination of these pivotal points in history was the bold abandonment of the RT/TT by many 'scholars,' pastors, and teachers. This resulted in the masses accepting and eating their false 'bread,' which is the *"lying words"* of man in the corrupted original language texts of Hebrew, Aramaic, and Greek, and the dynamic, or functional equivalent translations, such as the NIV, NLT, NASB, Message, etc.

Formal, verbal, plenary translations of the Hebrew Masoretic Text and the Greek Received Text were disdained. Eugene Nida was the principle individual responsible for the abandonment of translations that were made to the glory of God, in favor of inferior translations written for the receptor.

Faith in God's promises of Preservation of His Contract (His Words) was abandoned. The subsequent efforts of man to foolishly honor God by the false premises of "message" preservation and DE translating has not produced a better world in which to live. As a matter of fact, surveys and stats reveal just the opposite. After a century of false texts and translations, the world finds itself in ever increasing dangers in every part of the earth. The conclusion of this author is that the neglect to heed God's warnings about changing His fixed Contract has:

1.   Freed man from moral behavior and as a result has accelerated fornication, lying, stealing, greed, and all the other despicable characteristics of man.

2.   Encouraged and emboldened homosexuals and atheists.

3.   Has resulted in cohabitation and other alternative lifestyles.

4.   Has placed man on the precipice of world-wide economic failure with all of its attendant consequences.

5. Has caused man to turn to drugs or sorceries (Gr. pharmakeia), which *"neither [they] repented of,"* as relief from the stresses created by abandonment of faith in a Holy God and His Words (Rev. 9:21).

As you dig deeper into the true cause of modern decadence, may the Lord bless your investigation of this significant topic and may your wisdom and understanding help others to grow into mature soldiers of the 'received' Gospel of the Lord Jesus Christ. Amen.

In Christ,
H. D. Williams, M. D., Ph.D.

INDEX

ABOUT THE AUTHOR

Dr. Williams was born in Ft. Pierce, Florida. He was saved at the age of fourteen at his local Baptist church under Pastor J. R. White where he was active in the church youth group. His local church ordained him to preach the gospel. After graduating with honors from high school, he attended Stetson University where he met his wife, Patricia, and they were married in 1961. Starting in the ministerial program at Stetson and switching to pre-med in his junior year, he graduated with honors with a B.A. After Stetson, he taught high school at Eau Gallie, Florida for two years, and then continued his training at the University of Miami Medical School where he graduated with honors. Following his medical training, Dr. Williams and Patricia settled in New Port Richey, Florida where he practiced Family Medicine as a board certified family practitioner. He was active in his community as a hospital board member for twenty years, a chief-of-staff, president of the medical society, an advisory board member and president of Moody Bible Institute's Florida program, a board member of the Health Planning Commission, and a teacher at his local Baptist church. He helped develop and administrate a multi-specialist medical clinic with forty thousand patients and seventeen doctors. His Biblical training was obtained at Stetson University, Moody Bible Institute, and Louisiana Baptist University. After retirement, Dr. Williams has continued serving the Lord Jesus Christ as an associate pastor, a teacher, and as vice-president and representative for the Dean Burgon Society. He received a Ph.D. in Biblical studies at Louisiana Baptist University. He has traveled to many foreign lands where he has represented the Dean Burgon Society, teaching pastors and participating in evangelistic events. He is author of the several books, *The Miracle of Biblical Inspiration; The Lie That Changed The Modern World; Word-For-Word Translating of the Received Texts, Verbal Plenary Translating; Hearing the Voice of God; The Septuagint is a Paraphrase; The Pure Words of God; The Attack on the Canon of Scripture, The Covenant of Salt; Wycliffe Controversies; The Accuracy and Faithfulness of the King James Bible,* in addition to many articles and booklets. Dr. Williams and his wife, Patricia have two sons, five grandchildren, and two great-grandchildren.

BOOKS BY DR. WILLIAMS

WORD-FOR-WORD TRANSLATING OF THE RECEIVED TEXT, VERBAL PLENARY TRANSLATING:

This 270 page perfect bound book may be purchased through Amazon.com or Barnes and Noble. There is a vital need for a book to inform sincere Bible-believing Christians about the proper techniques of translating the WORDS of God into the receptor languages of the world. No book like this one has ever been written. It is a unique and much-needed book. The very first requirement for any translation of the Bible is to have the proper WORDS of Hebrew, Aramaic, and Greek from which to translate. It is the contention of this book that the original verbally and plenarily inspired Hebrew, Aramaic, and Greek WORDS have been verbally and plenarily preserved in accordance with God's promises. These preserved WORDS are those received-text-WORDS which underlie the King James Bible. This volume emphasizes the requirement of a proper technique to be used in all translations of God's WORDS. It must be done in a verbally and plenarily translation technique. That is, the Hebrew, Aramaic, and Greek WORDS must be conveyed into the receptor languages, not merely the ideas, concepts, thoughts, or message. This technique is absent in all of the other manuals on Bible translation. Dr. Williams is not the usual sort of writer. He combines the meticulous skill of a Doctor of Medicine with the artistry and acumen of a Doctor of Philosophy to produce this grand volume. May translators and sincere Christians of all persuasions and professions use this important book worldwide! It is available at Amazon.com. (type in book title) or Barnes and Noble.com and in the bookstore at:

www.theoldpathspublications.com

THE ATTACK ON THE CANON OF SCRIPTURE, A POLEMIC AGAINST MODERN SCHOLARSHIP

This 172 page perfect bound book was released in January, 2008. ISBN 978-0-9801689-0-7. This book demonstrates the newest attack on the Words and books of the Bible by modern day scholarship. The changing methods for assaulting the Scriptures are important for those who are concerned about the relentless attempt to destroy them. In a remarkable polemic against modern scholarship, Dr. Williams outlines the most recent means many are using to undermine confidence in the Words of God received through the priesthood of believers. It is available at Amazon.com. (type in book title) or Barnes and Noble.com and in the bookstore at:

www.theoldpathspublications.com

THE LIE THAT CHANGED THE MODERN WORLD

This book is in perfect bound format, 440 pages in all. ISBN 1-56848-042-3. It is a factual defense not only of the King James Bible, but also of the Hebrew and Greek Words that underlie the King James Bible. The historical material is approached in a detailed manner, like a doctor would approach an epidemiological study. The work demonstrates the attack on Scripture by individuals through the centuries and the changes, additions, and subtractions from Biblical manuscripts. Examples are given. Furthermore, the results or application of the devastating effects are discussed. The author is a medical doctor, now retired, who has researched this important topic thoroughly. May the Lord Jesus Christ use and honor this study in the days, weeks, months, and years ahead until our Lord Jesus Christ returns. It should be in every layman's library, every Pastor's library, every church library, every college library, every university library, and in every theological seminary library. It is available at Amazon.com. (type in book title) or Barnes and Noble.com and in the bookstore at:

www.theoldpathspublications.com

THE PURE WORDS OF GOD

This is a perfect bound 136 page book. ISBN 978-0-9801689-1-4. Dr. Williams' book, *The Pure Words of God,* clarifies the use of the word "pure" when it is used to define the Words of God. Should "pure" be applied to translations, to Traditional/Received Texts, or to Critical Texts? Once the correct application is explained, Dr. Williams clarifies God's commands to receive and keep His pure Words. It is available at Amazon.com. (type in book title) or Barnes and Noble.com and in the bookstore at:

www.theoldpathspublications.com

WYCLIFFE CONTROVERSIES

This 311 page perfect bound book is about Dr. John de Wycliffe (1324?-1384). He is an important person in the history of the Bible and Bible Translating. This book is an attempt to recognize and place in one book the contradictions and confusion surrounding Wycliffe and his colleagues. For example, are the Wycliffe Bible Versions based upon Old Latin Texts close to the received Text or are they closer to Alexandrian Texts that influenced Jerome's Latin Vulgate? In addition, many other questions have been raised in the literature such as who were Wycliffe's close associates who participated in the work; where and when did the Lollards that were associated with him originate; and many other controversies. Dr. Williams provides some evidence for most likely answers to a number of questions. It is a perfect bound, 311 pages. It is available at Amazon.com. (type in book title) or Barnes and Noble.com and in the bookstore at:

www.theoldpathspublications.com

HEARING THE VOICE OF GOD

This 311 page perfect bound book discusses the critical factors related to the postmodern confusion surrounding this issue. The subject is clearly and realistically approached from a plenary Biblical approach. Mysticism accompanying this issue is refuted. This work investigates the topic as it relates to revelation, conscience, inspiration, illumination, and the voice of the Lord in Scripture. Dr. Williams explains how postmodern philosophy has created an atmosphere that contributes to the confusion surrounding this issue. It is available at Amazon.com. (type in book title) or Barnes and Noble.com and in the bookstore at:

www.theoldpathspublications.com

TIIE KING JAMES BIBLE'S ACCURACY AND FAITHFULNESS; A Celebration; Historical Quotes About the KJB.

"Dr. Williams has rendered a great service to all students of the King James Bible. His masterful historical research demonstrates that there have always been critics of the King James Bible but their criticisms are willful and not scholarly. Genuine scholars have repeatedly risen to its defense and promotion. They still do. This book is a great resource in the study of the history of the King James Bible. I recommend it to any serious student of the King James Bible." It is available at Amazon.com. (type in book title) or Barnes and Noble.com and in the bookstore at:

www.theoldpathspublications.com

THE COVENANT OF SALT

The use of the word "salt" in Scripture has been interpreted in many different ways over the centuries. Many have complained of the difficulty understanding the meaning of salt found in various passages. Just as leaven has a consistent meaning throughout the Bible, this book reveals the usual typological meaning of salt as the Words of God.

As this book also explains, salt is related to the Words of God, preservation of the Words of God, the Lord Jesus Christ, and the Covenant. There is a significant interrelationship.
If:

- The Covenant = the Lord Jesus Christ (Isa. 42:6)
- The Covenant = the Words of God (Old and New Testament)
- Salt = the Words of God (Old and New Testament)
- Then: Salt = the Lord Jesus Christ.

It is available at Amazon.com. (type in book title) or Barnes and Noble.com and in the bookstore at:
www.theoldpathspublications.com

THE MIRACLE OF BIBLICAL INSPIRATION
There are numerous opinions in the literature concerning the meaning of "inspiration" of the Bible such as "the partial view," "the natural view," "the neoorthodox view," "the pagan view," and many others. The explanation of most of the various views is very troubling. Very few positions exalt the true origin of the original Words of the Bible in Hebrew, Aramaic, and Greek. The positions fail to correctly recognize that the process and the product of "inspiration" is a miracle "once delivered." Inspiration is a very TECHNICAL term. Dr. Williams' work will help others to understand the meaning of the words associated with "inspiration" in their Biblical context.
"And that from a child thou hast known the holy scriptures, which are able to make thee wise unto salvation through faith which is in Christ Jesus.". 2 Timothy 3:15
"All scripture is given by inspiration of God, and is profitable for doctrine, for reproof, for correction, for instruction in righteousness:" 2 Timothy 3:16
"For the prophecy came not in old time by the will of man: but holy men of God spake as they were moved by the Holy Ghost." 2 Peter 1:21
"But there is a spirit in man: and the inspiration of the Almighty giveth them understanding. Great men are not always wise: neither do the aged understand judgment." Job 32:8-9
It is available at Amazon.com. (type in book title) or Barnes and Noble.com and in the bookstore at:
www.theoldpathspublications.com

Articles by Dr. Williams and ebooks can be found at:
www.theoldpathspublications.com

www.ingramcontent.com/pod-product-compliance
Lightning Source LLC
Chambersburg PA
CBHW051840090426
42736CB00011B/1903